Early Acclaim for
LIFE BEYOND BELIEF

Alice welcomes us to the simple wonder of what is, to the effortless Self that is always present behind every thought, every action. This is a journey from mind to heart, from separation to oneness. Follow its thread, because these are words that can open what is closed, free what is imprisoned, and help you to live awake.

LLEWELLYN VAUGHAN-LEE, Ph.D., Sufi teacher and author of *Working with Oneness* (www.workingwithoneness.org).

I love this book! It is down to earth and essential—where heaven and earth meet!

GANGAJI, spiritual teacher and author of *The Diamond in Your Pocket, Discovering your True Radiance, You are That* and *Freedom and Resolve* (www.gangaji.org)

In this wide-ranging account rooted in profound personal experience, Alice Gardner takes the reader on a jour͏ penetrating significance. It ends up where all such jo͏ inevitably invite us to travel—deep into the lived exp͏ of love. Thus, she provides a wonderful guidebook͏ own such journey.

MARK BRADY, Ph.D., author of *A Little Book of Parer* and *The Wisdom of Listening.*

Alice Gardner has succeeded brilliantly in breathing her humanity into the story of awakening to 'what is.' Throughout the book, she points out the universality of the cross-cultural perennial Truth that everything is, quintessentially, only One. By directly encouraging us to actively use whatever experiences show up as an occasion to deepen our awareness, she short-circuits the mind's proclivity to separate itself from the heartbeat of Life. Clear, personal and very readable. Highly recommended.

CHUCK HILLIG, MFT, author of *Enlightenment for Beginners, Looking for God: Seeing the Whole in One, Seeds for the Soul, The Way IT Is*, and *The Magic King* (www.chuckhillig.com).

Alice Gardner's personal touch creates a bond with the reader. She leads you from exactly where you are—physically, emotionally, spiritually—through layers of beliefs, programming, and conditioning, to a place of accessible freedom. You don't have to go to a monastery. You don't have to get divorced. You don't have to go on a diet. You don't have to do anything other than follow this book's pointers into the current thoughts, feelings and circumstances of your already existent life.

The writing style is breezy and calm, organized and focused, and at the same time revelatory and demanding. Gardner is an excellent person to take you into the world of radically honest spirituality. Go with her on a journey of discovery in Life Beyond Belief.

JERRY KATZ, editor of *One: Essential Writings on Nonduality* (www.nonduality.com).

This book offers important guidance for people who want to realize their true spiritual nature while living active, productive lives. Gardner's down-to-earth voice and her honesty about her own challenges and limitations make it enjoyable, accessible reading.

JUDITH BLACKSTONE, Ph.D., educator, psychotherapist, and author of *The Empathic Ground, Living Intimately and The Enlightenment Process* (www.realizationcenter.com).

Life Beyond Belief is a well-written and accessible guide to awakening from the dominion of the ego to the Heart of Life. Alice Gardner writes in a personal, honest and sometimes humorous manner that reflects the joy of living in the present moment.

KATIE DAVIS, spiritual teacher and author of *Awake Living Joy* (www.katiedavis.org).

Alice Gardner points to a spirituality that does not depend on belief or dogma. It bridges all barriers in an age where spirituality is divided according to beliefs that only create more separation. She brings it back home to the moment-to-moment experience of our daily lives and the immediacy of our own direct experience beyond all beliefs.

Spirituality has historically been about getting away from or transcending our daily life experience. Alice Gardner's practical offering of life beyond our beliefs puts spirituality back into its rightful place, at the center of what is happening each moment in our day-to-day life.

LYNN MARIE LUMIERE, MFT, psychotherapist, co-author of *The Awakening West* and contributing author to *The Sacred Mirror: Non-dual Wisdom and Psychotherapy.*

After thousands of years of teachings that point to the Truth of Being, it appears that now is the time for teachings on how to live the Truth of Being. Whether you have experienced just a glimpse of who you really are, or whether you know who you really are, Life Beyond Belief offers a wise and compassionate companion on the journey to now live who you really are.

CAROL SCHIRA MA, LMFT, psychotherapist., director of the Couples Resource Center.

...Alice writes this book from a heart, mind and body wholeness.

RITA KAUFMAN, RSM and spiritual director.

Alice Gardner brings exquisite awareness of the opportunities life provides for self-examination. In this lucid book she takes us to the edge of our own traditions so that we may glimpse a universal question for those of us attempting to hold to a spiritual path: How are we to practice during the daily activities of life? Gardner offers, gently, an answer: Take those activities as the kindling for the fire of personal transformation. Wonderfully written. Biographical of the human condition. I highly recommend this book!

RYAN ROMINGER, Ph.D. in Transpersonal Psychology, spiritual director and adjunct faculty at the Institute of Transpersonal Psychology.

Life Beyond Belief

Life Beyond Belief

Everyday Living as Spiritual Practice

Alice Gardner

Awake Publishing

Stanford, California

Awake Publishing
Stanford, California
USA
www.awakepublishing.com

Life Beyond Belief:
Everyday Living as Spiritual Practice

Cover design and author photograph: Lyn Carr
Text design: Wahmpreneur Books
Cover photograph: Alice Gardner
Editing: Priya Irene Baker and John B. Gardner

Printed in the United States of America.

ISBN 978-0-9792435-0-9

LCCN: 2007906003

The following publishers and authors have generously given
permission to use previously published material:

Adyashanti, for excerpts from *My Secret is Silence* and
Impact of Awakening. Copyright 2000 & 2003 by
Adyashanti. Reprinted by permission of Adyashanti and
Jerilyn Munyon.

Coleman Barks, for "The Guest House" and two excerpts
from "The Music Master" found in *The Essential Rumi*.
Copyright 1995 by Coleman Barks, reprinted by permission
of Coleman Barks.

Eckhart Tolle, for excerpts from *The Power of Now*.
Copyright 1997 in Canada by Eckhart Tolle. Reprinted by
permission of Namaste Publishing and New World Library.

"Watch the dust grains moving
in the light of the window.

Their dance is our dance.

We rarely hear the inward music,
but we're dancing to it nevertheless,

directed by the one who teaches us,
the pure joy of the sun,
our music master."

Rumi, "The Music Master" [1]

Acknowledgements

I wish to thank all those whose lives have converged with my own to stimulate the writing of this book, especially Eckhart Tolle, Adyashanti, Dorothy MacLean and Richard Moss but also the many others too numerous to mention who inspired me along the way. The seeds planted by your lives and work have sprouted and are growing and strong.

I also wish to thank my family for their support in this project, especially the editorial assistance given by my father, but also the overall support of my whole family who believed I could do it and stood behind me. I would like to thank my two children, Tara and Derek who cheered me on in my explorations at a time when they could have easily have wished for a more "normal" Mom.

Thank you all for your Love, wisdom, support and encouragement.

TABLE OF CONTENTS

FOREWORD by M.B. Handspicker, Ph.D xix

INTRODUCTION 1

SECTION 1:

PERSONAL STORY/UNIVERSAL STORY

Chapter 1: The Value of Our Stories 12

Chapter 2: Alice's Story 22

SECTION 2:

THE UNIVERSAL PROCESS OF AWAKENING

Chapter 3: What is Awakening? 38

Chapter 4: Living from Awakeness in a World of Duality . 46

Chapter 5: Always and Already Awake 54

Chapter 6: Letting Life Live 60

SECTION 3:

AFTER THE REALIZATION

Chapter 7: Our Conditioning and How It Clears Itself 72

Chapter 8: Identity and Self-Centered Living 78

Chapter 9: Conditioning in Relationships 84

Chapter 10: Conditioning Around Spirituality 94

Chapter 11: Mind as Servant 99

SECTION 4:

TROUBLESHOOTING THE LIVING OF THIS

Chapter 12: Believing Your Thoughts 108

Chapter 13: Referencing Other People for Reality 112

Chapter 14: Reclaiming Lost Parts of Ourselves 117

Chapter 15: Adopting the Whole Process into
Our Separate Identity 126

Chapter 16: Choosing Truth over Comfort 129

Chapter 17: Mind's Basic Control Strategy 135

Chapter 18: Nowhere to Stand 141

SECTION 5:

IS THERE AN END TO THE PROCESS?

Chapter 19: Ending and Beginning, All At Once 148

Chapter 20: Completion and Incompletion
Enjoying Each Other 152

SECTION 6:

LOVE BEYOND BELIEF

Chapter 21: Love as the One That is Everywhere 162

Chapter 22: Love Beyond Reason 166

Afterword 177

Notes 181

Selected Bibliography 186

About the Author 189

Foreword

While working on a project establishing an Interfaith Council in a small, diverse college in Vermont, I first met Alice Gardner. My path has been as a Christian theologian, a staff member of an international ecumenical organization, and a professor at Andover Newton Theological School. In these roles I have been able to provide many people with guidance and support as they sought out a meaningful spiritual life and as they prepared to aid others in that search as ministers. I was pleased to be asked to read this book. I was *delighted* when I finished reading it. It fills a needed niche in the bourgeoning spiritual literature of today: the spirituality of everyday life. Already it has helped shape my own practice. I can commend it to others on the basis of that experience and its appeal across spiritual and religious divides.

In this book Gardner clearly draws on Eastern traditions but writes as a child of the West (not as an imitator of the East). There are many points where the resonances to biblical tradition are evident to me in her writing, allowing easy substitution of my own Christian vocabulary for the reality she describes. For instance, her description of the "mind-made" version of ourselves and the difficulties it causes us, translates beautifully into the Christian tradition. (Paul struggles with the problem in Romans 7. "I do not understand my own actions. For I do not do what I want, but I do the very thing I hate.") Awakening to our authentic selves puts the mind-made persona in its proper place—as the servant of the self rather than its master. This same transformation is called for in the Gospel tradition where Jesus says, "Those who find their life will lose it, and those who lose their life for my sake will find it." (Matthew 10:39) I suspect people from other religious traditions could easily do the same. Gardner writes in a mystical tradition that historically has transcended the boundaries of the various faith communities, uniting us in the commonality of our everyday life experiences.

Frithjof Schuon describes this kind of boundary-crossing in his book, *The Transcendent Unity of Religions*[1]. He posits that the various revealed religions are diverse pointers to a divine reality that transcends them all. As Huston Smith observes in his introduction to Schuon's book: "Forms are to be transcended by fathoming their depths and discerning their universal content, not by circumventing them. One might regard them as doorways to be entered, or rather as windows, for the [mystic] doesn't leave them behind, but continues to look through them toward the Absolute...

---

[1] Frithjof Schuon, The Transcendent Unity of Religions. Wheaton, Illinois: The Theosophical Publishing House, 1993.

The [mystic] finds the Absolute within the traditions as poets find poetry in poems." [2]

It is in the context of such an understanding that Gardner's work is so important. She sees our traditions and religions as our servants and not our masters: they are asked to both support and challenge us in every circumstance of our ordinary lives.

As knowledge of diverse traditions increases, there is more and more "borrowing" amongst them. Huston Smith, a devout Methodist, nevertheless engages in more than one spiritual practice he learned from his study of Eastern traditions. Trappist monks in Massachusetts had a Zen master teach them meditation. A Dominican priest wrote a book on "Christian Yoga." My own pastor is a yoga practitioner and takes retreats at meditation centers periodically. It is clear that many religious people in the West discover that practices from the Eastern traditions are helpful to them. The goal is to weave together whichever practices are fruitful for each unique individual in such a way that they provide us with integrity and coherence.

Love is the ultimate nature of reality for Gardner, and therefore the actuality of our authentic self—even when we do not realize it. All the processes she describes as functioning naturally in daily life are

---

[2] Ibid., p.xxv.

designed by Love to open us to this reality not only in fact but in function.

Gardner's very title, "Life Beyond Belief," gives an important perspective on belief in a time of fundamentalisms and ideologies functioning as idols in human life. Her experience points out that belief is a shallow substitute for the actual experiencing of the divine in the midst of life. No matter what our spiritual leanings, she invites us into to a way of living that connects us with the divine at work in our own daily experience.

M.B. Handspicker, Ph.D.
Professor of Pastoral Theology, Emeritus
Andover Newton Theological School, Newton, MA

Introduction

Is it possible to live a spiritually awakened life without withdrawing from the world? This book affirms that it is not only possible but that it is a crucial step being called for by our world situation, our times, and the deepest place in our hearts. This book is written from my vantage point of being an ordinary person who has been using her own life as a laboratory to explore in this territory for over thirty years. In this book I present my experience so far, along with commentary on how I see the implications for all of us.

Past generations of people seeking to penetrate the secrets of spiritual identity and the source of human suffering have isolated themselves from the world in order to pursue this work, creating an environment of peace within which to uncover the spiritual treasure of their inner beings. We also see many modern people relating to religion and spirituality in superficial ways by simply paying tribute to the divine once a week, on special occasions or when problems occur, not knowing how to connect with this source of divine nourishment more fully in the midst of their frenetically busy modern lives. In either solution, people can often find themselves tightly held within strict systems of beliefs that allow them to feel that their way is right and that the results are good enough or are all that is possible.

This book is asking: is it really possible to live a life that isn't constrained by tightly held beliefs about who we think we are and what is possible for us? Is it really possible to speak and act with freedom and integrity in all that we do, becoming clear channels of expression for authentic selves rooted in our essential core of divine Love?   The main offering of this book is the suggestion that, yes, a way is becoming open for us to live our deepest spiritual truths right in the middle of whatever circumstances we have been given in our down-to-earth lives. The invitation is that we may become explorers together in this territory. While you are reading, please use your own personal experience and perspectives alongside mine in order to see how best to embody this possibility in your own life.

Inspired spiritual teachers have been telling us in so many different ways that we are not who we thought we were. We are not the bundle of ideas and beliefs that we hold in relation to ourselves. We are being told that we are something quite else, something wonderfully beyond our old beliefs, something free and vital and awake. Perhaps we may know this firsthand in our personal experience or maybe we simply hear it and can feel its truth resonate within us. In either case, we often find ourselves inexplicably wanting the full experience of this more than anything. We want so much to connect with this deeper source of nourishment in life. The real possibility of awakening seems to be available to normal everyday people now, and in greater numbers than ever before. I am an example of that. A door is open now that has before been closed. Perhaps we owe a debt to the work of all of the previous generations for this happy circumstance. For whatever reason, we seem to now have a double opportunity available to us that has not been as accessible to people in the past: to simultaneously be accessing our deeply spiritual nature and also to be living active lives in the world.

Not only is spiritual enlightenment, as Eckhart Tolle would call it, now a possibility for people involved in worldly life but it actually seems that now it is advantageous to our spiritual lives to be active in the world. To retreat to a mountaintop, either real or proverbial, would be to avoid our deepest and most critical work: that of becoming a clean, clear vehicle for the divine energy to use as a portal through which to enter into the world in a new way. Our worldly circumstances now are supporting us in allowing ourselves to be used by life in a way that retreating to a mountaintop would prevent. This book uses my own experience as an entryway into the subject, because of course it was my entryway, but then goes on to inquire into what the implications of this might be for all of our lives. The full answer to that inquiry lies entirely with you and your willingness to also explore.

Spiritual practice for many people has meant adding time-consuming rituals and exercises of all sorts to our daily lives to help us keep focused, to nurture our spiritual nature, to quiet the mind or to open ourselves to new perceptions of reality. While these practices in many cases can still be beneficial, this book presents a type of spiritual practice that is not added on to daily life, but is already integrated as a part of it. It talks about using the actual content of whatever is already happening in our life experience, no matter what that content is, in a way that invites us to notice both in ourselves and in our circumstances the most perfect spiritual teaching imaginable. If we can accept the perfection of life as it already is, and really listen to the things that we would otherwise have labeled as wrong or bad, then we can begin to see that our circumstances are exactly what we need, to do the work that we are here to accomplish in our lifetime.

Unlike many books containing pure spiritual instruction, this book is written from a personal vantage point even though in an absolute sense, that which we awaken to is not personal at all. This is because I am wishing to honor the human part in all of us. There has been so much said in spiritual literature about how our down-to-earth lives are not real and are illusory. These kinds of statements cause us to think that gaining access to non-dual awareness is the whole of awakening, but from my own experience this awakening is part of something larger. Spiritual awakening is a beginning rather than the end that we have so often been taught that it is. It surprised me to find, after my own awakening had miraculously occurred, that there still remained a definite ability for my behaviors to be generated by the antics of my conditioned self, even though I was no longer totally identifying with that version of self. I was surprised to see that! I had not been prepared to see this corruptibility in myself though in hindsight I think I could easily have noticed it in others.

In order to fully live the truth that awakening brings us in contact with, there needs to be a relaxing of the conditioning in our mental bodies and the wounds in our emotional bodies. Only then can we hold this realization in a healthy way, express it cleanly in the realm of everyday life and fully embody it. This process is available to us through the circumstances that our daily life provides, and as such, is equally available both before and after awakening. Awakening itself may not necessarily appear to be a radical change point but may slide in quietly when we are not noticing.

Our imperfect humanness does not impede our ability to embody and live the wholeness of our true nature. These human-being suits and their stories actually support, enhance and enrich our true nature tremendously if we can have the humility to recognize the gifts that they bring us. The human part of who we are is a miracle in itself, and must not be discounted when it is called unreal or illusory, even though that may be true in an absolute sense. It is a great privilege and miracle to be here in our physical/mental/emotional bodies and also be able to access the fullness of what we really are at the same time, to whatever extent we are able. In that is a holiness that is beyond words. The point is to be a bridge, so that our spiritual realization touches down into ALL that it is to be human. We need our bodies, our minds, our jobs, our families, our loved ones, our difficulties and our circumstances in order to be this bridge.

Knowing spiritual truths is one thing. Living them fully is quite another. While it is wonderful to meet who we really are behind our conditioning and to see life for what it is, it is my experience that this is only one part of a multi-faceted process. The larger process is about letting our realization enter every aspect of our human nature so that the flavor of the divine moves through us in the midst of every kind of circumstance, comfortable or not. Our realizations are not end points allowing us to find peace through detachment from life. Life wants us in the midst of it! We seem to be moving towards making our beloved Earth uninhabitable if we do not bring this newly available awareness and energy down into our work places, our homes and families, our enemy-making processes and our difficulties with people who disagree with us.

There are numerous teachings and teachers today who speak to us so beautifully and clearly about spiritual enlightenment, awakening, divine love and other such things. These beautiful teachings can stimulate people to experience elevated spiritual states that can seem to come and go and that don't remain accessible upon returning home to earn a living or relate to our families. This can feel like an in-and-out process of being awakened and then having it taken away. This book offers that the cause of this in-and-out feeling lies in the way that we approach the problems and obstacles in our down-to-earth lives, not the fact that they exist. If we can stay open to the possibility that any unpleasant thing that life might throw at us is the perfect thing to have happening right then, then *all* of our life can begin to serve our awakening in amazing ways. The unpleasant feelings can show us what we need to put our attention on in our inner constructions—what we need to look into. The difficulties that always looked as if they were in the way of our spiritual growth become the way forward for us now, helpfully bringing us information on what we need to look into for release from our conditioned thinking and our emotional wounding.

This book was originally written for the most part in the mornings before going to work at a very busy full-time job and on the weekends over a four month period. My personal engagement with aspects of the material resulted in the writing of each chapter. Synchronistic things would happen in my days that were so obviously connected to the morning's writings. It is clear that I lived this book as it was written and that writing it has propelled me into an even more personal integration of this material as I write, edit, read and re-write, and keep opening up my ability to say it more clearly, and live it more fully.

It is important to keep in mind that everything in this book is coming through my own filters and lenses and therefore needs to be tested in the context of your own lives. I can make no claims to a lack of such filters. I am a fallible human being like the rest of us. Although I did have a distinct awakening in 2002 and remain in touch with who I truly am since that time, I am still working, now in the deep emotional roots that caused the mind-made-self to develop in the first place. I write from the midst of the process being described, hopefully offering some perspective along the way, and not from any end point. Please take what is of value to you from my experience and find your own way.

Though patterns of similarity between people do exist, there is no right way or wrong way to wake up. Everyone is different. The elements and the ordering of the awakening process will not follow my example but will instead reflect the way that you are particularly put together. Please make up your own mind about everything here. Do not take my word for anything. Decide for yourself if any of it is true for you. This is of vital importance. Take no one else's truth for your own truth. Both teachers and companionship on the spiritual path are wonderfully helpful at certain junctures, but essentially you must find your own way through your own unmapped inner territory. Your journey through this terrain will undoubtedly be as unique as you are, and although we can broaden our perspectives by listening to each other, we must find our own way to our unique expression of this awakeness for ourselves. Although I do generalize about my own experiences in this book as being equivalent to the human experience, I need to say that I am not a therapist and am not familiar with scenarios involving mental illness, criminality and so on, and don't know how what I have written may or may not apply to those particular situations.

I see clearly the limitations inherent in spiritual books and the way that they can sometimes even be used to postpone the actual events of awakening by keeping that awakening at a distance and not allowing it to come into the actual details of real lives. I am hoping that because this book is about the process of bringing your realization into the midst of everyday life that it will not be used to create distance, but this is really up to you the reader. Towards this end I write as a fellow human being, not as an elevated soul or a disembodied voice offering wisdom to the world. Books have served me as wonderful catalysts in my life and were the closest thing to tapping into humanity's collective experience through those who wrote books, and I am forever grateful for the trouble that the authors took to do so. Books were particularly important when I didn't have people in my community who understood what was happening with me. This was particularly true for years after my own awakening in 2002 when I still lived in rural Vermont. This experience, and a general feeling of wishing to pass on this experience of awakeness in any way I can, has helped motivate writing and offering this book and also my website at www.wideawakeliving.com to others who might enjoy it and possibly gain perspective on their own journeys from what it contains.

Section 1

Personal Story/Universal Story

"From this oneness, individuality can be celebrated."
Adyashanti [2]

It is a vital developmental stage for us to accept our humanity fully and to no longer resist it as if it were in our way en-route to our transcendent perfection.[3]

Even though they are not true in the absolute sense, our stories bring us into alignment with what is true by cycling us through the world of experience in ways that are set-ups to unlock and awaken whatever is not yet awake in us. It is not just a matter of whether the stories are true or not, it is a matter of whether we are willing to see what they are offering us, which takes great humility.

Chapter 1

The Value of Our Human Stories

A common viewpoint among spiritually oriented people holds that our life stories are either illusory dreams or are problematic distractions keeping us from fully living a spiritual life. This view may come from books that we have read or from what we have been told. It also may very likely come from the way we experience our lives. There is often a striking difference between how we feel in the midst of our spiritual practice (whatever form that may take) and how we feel at work, in the midst of our families or in the morning traffic. We conclude that the comfort of a quiet period of prayer or meditation is a spiritual experience and shows us that we are on the right track, while the discomfort of our responses to a stressful day at the office, or a child's tantrum, is a sign that we are not the spiritual person that we had hoped to be.

An alternate view will be offered here that has grown out of what seems obvious to me as I look at the world and at myself. I see that accepting our down-to-earth human aspects as part of the overall divine perfection is a vital part of being able to live in integrity with our authentic spiritual selves. This is not to argue with the viewpoint that our humanity has seemed to consist of illusory elements: ideas, stories, and mental interpretations of reality. I propose however that the human aspects of who we are encompass those illusory elements but also include important and sacred pieces of our wholeness that need to be embraced rather than excluded. I am seeing that it is a vital developmental stage for us to accept our humanity fully and to no longer resist it as if it were in our way. It seems that we are being now called upon to accept the human aspects of ourselves into the perfection of life as it is. The wholeness of being human is not just about the absolute truth of our spiritual identity, but also includes the activities of our physical, mental, and emotional bodies. It is only our previous resistance to being human in those ways that has made them seem to be blocking our development as spiritually awake beings. This book is an invitation to a way of living where our spiritual life is actually to be found within both the comforts and the discomforts of living all aspects of our daily lives in the midst of the world.

Even though they are not true in the absolute sense, our stories offer us the opportunity of bringing us into alignment with what is absolute and true by cycling us through the world of experience in ways that are set-ups to unlock and awaken whatever is not yet awake in us. It is not just a matter of whether the stories are true or not, it is a matter of whether we are willing to see what they are offering us, which takes great humility.

One way that we resist the opportunities of our humanness is when we yearn to give up our active personal lives and isolate ourselves from the world by perhaps entering a monastic community or living anywhere where we can be relatively undisturbed in our pursuit of spiritual truth (mountaintops and caves spring to mind). This is certainly an appropriate response at certain times for certain people but it seems that it often becomes an avoidance of a richer set of lessons. The intensity of modern life provides us with signposts leading to whatever is internally calling out for resolution within us. Do we really believe that spiritual states which can be achieved under a controlled outer environment but lost again in the fire of everyday living are enough? It seems to me that our twenty-first century world situation is calling for us to realize our spiritual nature and then to ground it in our humanness so that we can be conduits for divine love to enter into the world through us. The very denseness of our supposedly lower human aspects then become essential elements in love's descent into the world and vital parts of who we are, not the impediments that we previously thought they were.

As you will see in my own story in the following chapter, I started out on the spiritual path looking for an escape from the existential pains of the human condition. I think this is a common beginning point for many spiritually oriented people. Then we come to a point in the process where we need to reassess what is true for us. If the spiritual life remains an escape strategy from the fullness of life, then we are not going to continue on when we are asked to bring our spiritual realizations back down into the areas of our lives that we have risen to avoid. A very good argument can be made for the advisability of working through those areas that we most wish to avoid first, before ascending into realizations of our true nature, to avoid being mired down at this point in the journey. But this is not always something that we can make conscious choices about, because how we unravel ourselves depends on how we are put together.

It is probably evident at this point that these are matters about which it is not easy to communicate, and I hope that what I have already said has not been confusing or obscure. In the hopes of establishing some basic vocabulary, let me attempt to clarify my references throughout this book to two different parts or levels of who we are. I talk about who we really are and call it the Self, the authentic self, awakeness, Love or our true nature. These words are attempting to point to our identity as a beingness or presence where all are One, but which also appears as the sacred core identity of our individual human life. What all these words refer to is our already and always awake inherent beingness that we uncover in the course of our spiritual lives as who we truly are.

There is also extensive reference in this book to the version of self that we create with our minds as soon as we develop cognitive ability when we are young, and I generally call it the mind-made self. As children, we follow the patterns taught to us by our parents or caregivers and develop layers of coverings over the authentic core of who we are, so that we can do our best to handle our family situations and try to please the grownups that sustain and protect us. These are strategies for getting what we need (and are about survival at their root) and they cover over the authentic self with a noisy overlay of thoughts and moods and reactive responses based on their content. At different times I call this inauthentic version of self the "me," the mind-made self, the ego, the personality or the strategic self. Although these terms may technically mean various things in other contexts, my way of using them is just to refer to this made-up version of who we are. This is the part of us that gets such bad press in spiritual literature but it is actually an important part of our human-beingness without which we would not be able to function very well in the world. The difficulty only comes if we are totally identified with this mind-mediated version of ourselves.

This version of us has been created as the mental story of our unique personhood, tying us together as a distinct separate entity including being born on a certain date, raised by particular parents, and having some very specific experiences along the way. At each moment along the way we have taken the details of what has been happening in our personal life story and made our own interpretation based on our already accumulated past experiences. We then apply these interpretations to the present, creating each new moment as an extension of the past. This habit of interpreting and assigning meaning to things from our interpretations is so very useful in practical matters and for sorting vast amounts of information in a way that doesn't overload our brains. It is a necessary and basic brain function but it has been going beyond what is helpful, like a runaway train. We have been using our brains in this interpretive way to try to fathom the big questions of life (like "who am I?" for starters) and mind just isn't able to do that effectively. It is just not capable of carrying out this function of reality-creation and because of that it has been providing us with a view of reality that is very much not so. As we become able to distinguish between its appropriate use (for practical matters and basic brain function) and its inappropriate use (as a mental intermediary in the pursuit of reality) we can begin to see how amazing and useful a tool it is when it stays within its actual capabilities and what trouble it causes when it goes beyond that.

It truly is a miraculous and remarkable thing to be a unique and separate human being, even though we have long paid for it by living in a mind-mediated world of insufficiency and suffering. How much more remarkable it is when we are now able to notice the process of self-creation that we have been engaged in. We are beginning to be able to see from a vantage point that is outside of that mind-made version of ourselves. This is an evolutionary milestone! Now, by some miracle, we finally have the opportunity to see the self-creation process at work, and without denigrating it in any way, to see our life story from beyond itself. This gives us new possibilities for living! We become able to live our lives from a vantage point of freedom and possibility, outside of the limiting structures of our mind's ideas about who we are. We can begin to see the world and everything that is happening in it as a continuous and perfect miracle that we have the incredible privilege to be a part of. We can accept being here fully! We can be awake in both the comedy and the tragedy of our humanness, not needing to escape or denigrate it in the least.

A common error that so many of us make is to believe that just because we made our personal stories up, that there is something wrong about the human part of us and with the stories that we have created and lived. It can be helpful to see that, in a way, each person's story is the story of humanity, seen through a particular and unique lens. We wouldn't say that our being a child was wrong just because we now can see things as an adult. We wouldn't say that living in caves was wrong, just because now we have invented houses. Our story is not a problem now that we are seeing it for what it is, thanking it for bringing us here and letting it take its rightful place in the present, within the fullness of our true nature.

Pause in your reading now and review your own story for a moment—look at the details of your life, of what has happened to your "me." Go back in your mind to the innocence of childhood, however far back you are able to remember, and see if you can notice how the "me" was being formed by the things that parents and others said about you, and by your reactions to what was going on around you. Look into how you interpreted what happened to that "me" and how you built it up as you went along, with layers of interpretation and added meaning. How did the world treat you and how did you respond to it? Look into it deeply enough to see if indeed it is true that you made it up as you went along, that you built your version of yourself and "what life is like" just as a child builds towers with a construction set. Don't take my word for it. Look into it for yourself and see if it's true.

Seeing how we have covered over our authentic self with layers of mental constructs about who we are is huge. Relaxing around realizing the truth of that is equally important because mind can easily reassert its sovereignty through judgment or interpretation. If you see that you are being hard on yourself in any way about the content of your life story so far, just notice whether the self-deprecating behavior is also part of the personal story that you have constructed. Interpreting is just an extension of the story. Judging oneself is just more mental activity—just more layering over the surface of what is real and true. The key is to relax while seeing judgments, past interpretations, and similar patterns that have, up until now, been habitual and automatic. The separate self is seen to be a constructed entity but it will not entirely go away and we don't want it to! It is needed as an important tool for living and as a sacred and integral part of the bridge that we become between earth and spirit. The job of the separate self, however, will now change. It will relax more because it is being released from a large part of the duties that it has carried up to this point including solving life's big questions, knowing what is happening all the time, and knowing what to do about that.

In spite of what we might have thought, our histories are perfect just as they are. Our personal stories have served us so very well, no matter what their content is, no matter how harshly mind may want to judge them. Our life stories have gotten us here, and that is a miracle in itself, even if it may have sometimes felt like a terribly difficult journey. Our stories have given us just the challenges and the blessings that we have needed, just when we needed them, in order to do what we have come here to do, or perhaps more accurately, to be who we have come here to be. These life stories have gotten us to this amazing point of being able more and more to access and live from our true nature, our authentic self, and to embrace the mind-made self as one of our most useful assets. Some miraculous process has occurred where the personal experiences of our history are offering us the opportunity to progress into an entirely new perspective on life.

When we were children we could not move directly into this way of seeing life without our first engaging extensively with life. We needed to build up this mind-based sense of identity and live in it for a while before we became able to see through it. Some kind of maturing has occurred from our excursion into this version of ourselves. It was a necessary excursion for us, and it has brought us here. For that we can give this whole human journey our gratitude and acceptance and we can, if we are ready, open ourselves to the richness of the life force that would have remained locked away if we were to reject the blessings that our everyday lives are offering us in each moment through our down-to-earth human circumstances.

This Moment

This moment, each moment,
life surrounds us in a circle of circumstances,
scenes, colors, thoughts, textures of mind and emotion
and then,
habit causes us
to imagine that we own This,
that This belongs to our own little life
separate from everything.
Actually we own nothing, quite the opposite...
All our lives together
belong to This.

Chapter 2

Alice's Story

I have always loved to hear the stories of how other people's lives have unfolded, especially when the stories are about an awakening process. People's personal stories have helped to expand my openness to a larger world beyond the limitations of my own ideas about what is and is not possible.

Please don't read the account that follows as implying that I am anyone special. The greatest value of this book is in the fact that I am an unexceptional person and therefore the possibilities that I talk about are available to anyone motivated to discover them for themselves. If you believe that my life is more fortunate than the lives of others because of some difference between us then you have missed the point. What we awaken to is what we are mutually, not something any of us retains for ourselves.

Since my teenage years, matters of the spirit were of primary interest. The separate personal "me" that was operative at that time grasped the idea of inner heavenly realms as the only escape (other than dying) from the painful childhood and adolescent inadequacies with which it was plagued. I saw spiritual development as a primary type of personal development, the ultimate self-enhancement. If I were to enhance my personal self in sufficiently deep and profound ways then spiritual benefits would be bestowed on me. It may sound silly verbalized this way, but when the idea is looked into truthfully, it is found to lurk, sometimes quite subtly, at the heart of a lot of spiritual thinking. This is not because we are inherently bad or damaged. It is because the one who wants to be spiritual has to be left behind in order to reveal our true identity. That personal "me" naturally wants to improve itself, and measures, discriminates, judges, exerts effort, etc. That is just the way it is and all it knows how to do.

This is often the only place to begin or so it still seems now. Back then, I was totally identified with what Eckhart Tolle [4] calls the "mind-made self." Like everyone else I knew, as a young child, it seemed obvious to me that my ideas about myself were who I was, and there was no question of anything beyond or outside of that. The fact that my thoughts and feelings were so changeable according to my moods or circumstances didn't cause me to doubt this logic. In hindsight, it certainly did give me extremely shifting sands on which to base my self-esteem and my acceptability as a person.

So this limited idea of "I" began being a spiritual seeker, and "I" began seeking out personality experiences that had the promise of taking "me" towards enlightenment. "I" practiced kundalini yoga with a passion. "I" meditated. "I" checked out gurus. "I" considered the ministry. By 1977 my seeking brought me to the Findhorn Foundation [5] in Scotland for what would turn out to be seven years, during which time I married and my children were born. Soon after arriving, I opened up to being able to "get guidance" from what the Findhorn community called my "higher self." Any question this small and inadequate "I" could frame would be answered from within by a wonderful source of wisdom and enlightened perspective. It was very much like having my own personal holy book that I could always open up to the perfect page for what I needed to know. This became a tremendous education for this mind-made self, as well as a constant offering of another way to live based on a higher perspective on all my questions, rather than my getting answers that told me what to do.

Then, sometime in the late 1980s, my "guidance" began telling me that it was time for me to outgrow the outmoded and somewhat schizophrenic guidance model. It said I needed to step into the realization that I was not the ignorant one who was asking the questions, but rather that I was the one who knew the answers. It was asking me to actually *be* what I at that time called my "higher self." The small I, still very much in charge, choked on this idea thoroughly. It was fine as a lofty idea that I might on some far-distant day in the future have the potentiality to be an enlightened being, but it was not at all acceptable to tell me that the person I've been living as all these years could bow out right now. That person was invested in being small, full of faults, humble, self-conscious and no better than anybody else, and was into keeping her head down and staying safe in that way. Such a personality was not welcoming to anything that sounded so grandiose. Not knowing what else to do, I obediently stopped asking for guidance but then turned away from spiritual matters and sunk myself into a difficult marriage and an overly busy lifestyle for a while.

In 2002, after recovering from my second marriage and after my parenting duties were becoming less overwhelming, I started purposely crossing paths with some "enlightened" people. The most significant of those was Eckhart Tolle, whom I had discovered by searching "living in the present" on amazon.com. I had somehow realized that I wasn't living in the present. Eckhart's writing very obviously was speaking to me with the voice of my own guidance and very much caught and held my attention because of that, and because I had never really heard the concepts in the *The Power of Now*[6] expressed quite so simply and beautifully before. I was lucky to be able to register for a retreat with him at the Omega Institute in October of 2002.

After spending those five days in retreat, listening to Eckhart and enjoying his presence, something was totally different. It was hard to put my finger on what it was. Things seemed upside down and inside out, but that didn't make sense. It was obvious that the spiritual seeker had come to the end of the road. It was palpably clear that there was nowhere else to go anymore. This felt very blissful and yet it was very disconcerting to the old identity structure, which wanted to know exactly what that meant. It was natural to look towards Eckhart as the source of this miracle and I felt immensely grateful, but it was obvious that he didn't have any idea about what was going on with me, didn't even know who I was, and hadn't personally done anything in relation to me. Yet somehow I knew that what the "I" had always wanted, in terms of spiritual seeking, was now received and the search was over.

That search, which had for so long been the core meaning of my existence, was no longer a part of my internal navigation system. It was simply gone. Also gone were all my old practical methods of goal setting and organizing to achieve mind-made goals over time—something I had been quite good at. I had no idea how to function without these basic mental components of my personality structure and now felt totally adrift. It was an unbelievably wonderful place to be adrift in, but the not knowing how to live and not knowing what I was doing seemed at first like they were problems. Over time what occurred was a long process of acclimation to this seemingly entirely new life. Instead of solving the problem of not knowing, I simply got used to living with not knowing and learned that I could still function that way. I will talk more about that later in the book.

At the same time, the "mind-made self" was still very active and kept making repeated attempts to place this experience, which I only later learned to call "awakening," within its own structures. It wanted to make the experience understandable in that self's own limited terms, to reduce it to being something that happened to the same old self. The small self desperately wanted ownership of the experience, as it had held ownership of all the life experiences previous to it. The trouble was that its efforts were visible now. They were able to be seen for what they were, a diminishment of something larger that was now also experience-able. This something was beyond the mind's capacity to grasp, so it couldn't be understood in the normal way. It was experienced as a process that had come to life in me, something with a life of its own outside of my old systems of identity creation, goal setting, planning, and so on. It was something radically different but with a familiar feel to it, as if this totally new life had always been there but had just dropped below the screen of awareness and now had reappeared. Over time I have realized that this seemingly new life was who I had always and already been.

Along with being able to see this about myself came a new view of the world and everything in it. At that time the feeling was of two separate experiences: one was the bliss at the core of my own being and one was the bliss of looking at everything with my eyes newly opened to the divine nature all around me. It felt like many of the filters that had previously been interfering with my ability to see clearly had been lifted and now I was able to see the true nature of the things in my world. I was falling in love with the objects around me all the time. Looking at a cup or a tree was equally awe-inspiring in the way that only an exceptional sunset might have been before. This ability to see more of the incredibleness of everyday things has never left, except by being covered over temporarily with noisy thinking. Interestingly this didn't at first seem to include people. My ability to see people in this way has been more slowly opening up and that is described in later chapters as a process of accepting the fullness of my own humanness more and more fully.

After many months of a totally bliss-filled existence, the process then started to take me step-by-step through an awareness of some very humbling content in my mind (which was still very busy). Habitual thought patterns, which for whatever reason had never been visible to me before, were rising to the surface. This process is continuing and keeps going in more deeply as if through a layering of content. I have come to call it the "clean-up".

By 2003, the personal self that had called itself by the first person "I" for nearly 50 years, was existing side by side with the newly visible process. The personal self desperately wanted to understand what was going on. Like a Zen koan[7] this was the perfect impossible task. The personal self understood at this point that this process was the awakening that it had been looking for. It had, after all, been well-educated. But the inability to locate its awakened identity and the complete transparency of what was generating this process confounded it entirely. It was a task that the personal self could not even understand, let alone accomplish and one at which it was doomed to fail.

As the intensity of the discomfort increased, the small "I" became increasingly frightened and threatened and was busy creating endless and hopeless scenarios about itself. Hunger, need, lack and insecurity were triggered, as were horror and humiliation about its previously unconscious behaviors. These scenarios at least temporarily kept the small I's attention on itself. My mind-made self had a long track record of holding its own attention through having things wrong with itself and unsuccessfully and endlessly problem-solving to improve itself. It was trying harder than ever but its efforts had never before been so visible, so out in the open. They also had never before been seen to be so hopeless and ridiculous.

All this occurred in a field of awareness that saw the mind's activities within a larger context and saw that what was happening was good even though it was uncomfortable. This field of awareness embraced and included all the ideas about the small me within the fullness, the holiness, the wholeness of itself. The larger process with a life of its own had called up all that needed to come to light, all that in each moment was obscuring what was really so.

There were habitual patterns of thought working and they repeatedly were returning awareness back to identification with the concepts around self, and it was obvious that these patterns were amplifying around fear. But in whom were these habitual patterns embedded? In whom was the fear occurring? Again and again the attention returned to this. More and more the attention returned to the unchanging nature of what these pictures arise from and fall back into. Attention seemed to naturally be pursuing what was unmoving, and relaxing the previous tendency to meld itself to whatever is moving and changing. Attention was viewing with increasing equanimity those things that had previously been seen as good or bad, higher or lower, wanted or not, enlightened or not. They are now seen as pairs that together are two sides of the same thing, each containing the other.

Out of the muck what has arisen is an awareness of awareness! It may sound like nothing, but this is what is not changing. This is what is here when all mental, physical and emotional objects are seen to be passing. This is the bedrock out of which the world arises, and into which it disappears. To know it, all that was ever needed was to stop running away from anything. All my resistances to what was here in each moment have simply had the power in each moment to veil this reality from my view.

There has been a progressively growing comfort with the new life. As I write, I am now four-and-a-half years into the living of it. A major factor in my being able to relax into this life and be comfortable with it has been a teacher named Adyashanti. [8] Somewhere at the end of 2003, I discovered his teachings online and found them to be totally relevant to what was happening with me. It seemed almost as if he knew me, that he was writing about my experience as if he knew it from inside. His teaching clearly named what had happened as "awakening" and went on to discuss how to live after that has occurred. He didn't give me a map of the territory, because one of the characteristics of this new way of living seems to be the lack of maps, but he let me feel that what was happening was normal and that it had happened to many other people before, and this made it much easier to relax. Adyashanti calls the process of learning how to live after awakening "embodiment" [9] and this was the important part of his impact on my life. He draws on his own experience and from his work with many people who come to him who are awakening in his teachings.

Embodiment is a process that takes some time, at least in my experience, because the recognition and change that occurs in the "awakening" moment is not instantly livable, but requires in most cases a reorientation to the world and a clean-up of our conditioning before one is able to live one's life from what has been realized. It's rather like being a baby again, when one has to learn all over how to live from a new source of identity. In my experience, the mental structures that supported the old way of living have not suddenly gone silent. They keep running until they can all be fully seen through. Embodiment is a good word for this process because it is a progression from the pure realization towards the total living of it in the world, in the busyness of our jobs, parenting, the health of our bodies, and so forth. In order to totally be living from this new source of identity we have discovered, we need to see through the interferences one by one. Further discomfort that may arise in this process doesn't seem to matter as much as uncomfortable things might have mattered previously. Each time new content arises for clearing, it is welcomed now, even if it is the seeing of our resistance to being welcoming. Everything is welcome now, even and especially whatever we most don't want to look at in ourselves.

One characteristic of my own experience of this new way of living is that I have had to totally reinvent how to navigate my way through life—how to know what to do in any moment. For the first few years, this was experienced as a kind of floating, without goals and without the old way of planning. It felt like just waiting to see what would happen next all the time. Without anywhere left to go, I felt like I was drifting, yet a lot happened that way. The most surprising thing was that I moved more than 3000 miles across the country and everything fell into place in the most amazing way, including finding a new job, home and so on. I guess one could say that it was all a wonderful lesson in not needing to plan everything out in the old way. Now there is a new stage occurring which involves using the mind again in this navigation process but in a different way. It is a matter of using mind instead of being used by it. It seems that mind is an incredible tool, and that after we have more or less weaned ourselves away from the old way of letting mind run our lives, we can begin to utilize it differently, as a tool in the hands of who we truly are.

So this is where I would like to leave "my story"—without an ending. The personal self is no longer dominating (in terms of where the identity is being drawn from) and yet it has not disappeared by any means. It is clear that it is still doing its personal self things, just like it always did, but that they are not being given the same importance as they had been before. They have been sidelined. In the center is an unmoving steadiness that is now felt to be who I am, and against which mind's antics flash and disappear. Life appears as a constant moving miracle, one moment to the next, incredible in its beauty and its perfection, and wonderfully radiant with divine Love even in the midst of the discomforts of everyday earthly life.

Home

Oh, miraculous good fortune
To be born into a time
Where all the suffering and wandering
Is finding its way Home
To the place of Love's inhabitance.

Such fortune to find here also
This One who has been coming with us
Up through all the generations.
With her ancient and familiar face—
Together we come to our completion.

None of our tears have been in vain
None of our lives wasted.
Together we are simply a long-ripening fruit
Ready, at last, to fall.

Section 2

The Universal Process of Awakening

"Because of an innocent misunderstanding you think that you are a human being in the relative world seeking the experience of oneness, but actually you are the One expressing itself as the experience of being a human being."

Adyashanti [10]

"Are you resisting your here and now? Some people would always rather be somewhere else. Their 'here' is never good enough. Through self-observation, find out if that is the case in your life. Wherever you are, be there totally."

Eckhart Tolle [11]

Chapter 3

What is Awakening?

Awakening is one of many terms that have been given in different cultures and in different time periods throughout the history of mankind for a process whereby we are either suddenly or gradually shifted out of living a life of separation and suffering and transported into a realization of unity and love. Religious traditions are filled with such occurrences. Christians may refer to this as being born again or reaching the kingdom of heaven, Buddhists may call it enlightenment, and other traditions have their own names for it.

Unfortunately most of the world's religions have historically treated such events in people's lives as something so completely out of the normal range of human experience that it has become removed from what we consider possible for our own humble lives. It could be that this was once a perfectly valid perspective. Perhaps at one time a person could not hope to have even a glimpse outside of the limitations of the mind-made self without spending a lifetime in a religious setting.

It does seem that for whatever reason (maybe due to the effect of the lifetimes spent by these good people throughout history) the situation has changed for our generation. Spiritual awakening seems now be more available to ordinary people living normal lives than it has ever been in the past.

Many religions teach people how to follow the path set forth by their prophets and mystics by telling us to follow the right instructions on how to live, how to worship or how to meditate in the hope that others might then have a chance at achieving such holiness. These may be helpful as guidelines, but often the instructions themselves are taken very literally so that the results which they were initially intended to bestow get forgotten in the pursuit of correctly following the precepts.

Sometimes these instructions for living would yield fruit in someone's consciousness but what is surprising is that awakening experiences don't necessarily seem to be coming more frequently to those who follow our great and ancient traditions. Awakening seems to be happening as often to people outside of those sets of instructions for how to live, worship or meditate. There appears to be some other factor, some inherent openness perhaps that some people have in these matters, which allows these sorts of experiential breakthroughs to happen in their lives.

What sort of breakthroughs are we alluding to? We are referring to realizing an altogether different source of identity for who we are (as opposed to who we thought we were) and embracing a completely altered relationship with worldly life on account of this realization. It is an ending of the rule of the mind over one's life and liberation from the demands that mind makes. These demands might still be audible, but are no longer dominant. The mind may still be making plenty of noise, but its noise is not automatically listened to as relevant or true. Mind is just doing what minds do, either trying to get in the way or trying to be helpful, but it is no longer assuming the task of establishing our identity or figuring out the bigger questions in life.

The mind-made identity from which we have drawn our sense of self up until the point of awakening is still there but it has lost its central place in our being. There is something else now that is living life. Something quite beyond words and quite mysterious has usurped that central inner spot from which you take your sense of identity. The shift feels subtle, at least it did in my case, but as the implications start to hit home, we realize the enormity of the change. The life that proceeds from this new identity is another life entirely from the old life story. It is not under the control of the mind-made self that had previously been taken as who we were. Life is instead being served by that mind-made self in practical ways, as we would use a tool.

Then the question may arise: is this a momentary change that is going to fade away, leaving you to return to your previous life to pick up where you left off? The mind-made self would very much like to make the awakening experience a part of its own personal life story. If it does that, then it can return to its central place. Awakening then might seem to become one more experience to add to its repertoire of wonderful experiences that have happened to it. But it is a very interesting question to ask "Where could the awakeness go?" There is really no place for it to go, ever. All we can do is re-bury it under our personality structures and pretend it is something within our stories. There actually and truly is nowhere for it to go. It is always and already what we really are.

Sometimes what people experience is an in-and-out process of being in touch with their true nature after they have first encountered it. This may be a tactic that the separate self takes in relation to the incomprehensible nature of what has been encountered, perhaps just keeping exposure to it to a minimum for a while in order to allow for acclimation to what is being seen. There is a tendency of mind to bury and re-bury its encounter with reality intermittently at first. We can watch this process in ourselves, knowing that whatever has a changeable quality is being generated from mind and what has the quality of steadiness and unchanging stability is what lies behind mind's screen.

We might choose to re-bury our true nature as a misguided play for safety and security. There is nothing safe and secure about how it feels when the nameless mystery begins to be in charge of your life! Mind-generated fears can run wild with this scenario and motivate a takeover. The old identity doesn't know what's going on most of the time and it takes a lot of getting used to for this to be at all comfortable. This is a time when support from like-minded people can be extremely helpful. The mind-made identity needs to learn to relax and let the true nature take its rightful place in the center of things. Then mind can serve, rather than rule. Then our personal self has become an instrument in the hand of that ineffable divinity which overflows with a Love that is completely outside of what the mind could ever conceive. The rest of this book is about the process of allowing this Love, which is actually Life itself, the space to do its work both in us and in the world through us.

Awareness

Awareness of thought rising and falling,
Awareness of particular thoughts,
Like the old "me" story of limitation and lack
Or the selfish concerns for the separate person
I thought I was,
The habitual effort to enhance that supposed self
somehow,
Or resist somehow being diminished.
The Buddhists call it well; desire and aversion.
Old habits appearing in a field of awareness,
Visible and absurd, no longer making sense in the old
way.
It was always hopeless before...
But now it is a joyous game to play if it serves delight
in life,
And serves, somehow, the emergence of the Real into a
world
So full of strife and struggle
So hoping for this Peace
Called the Peace "that passeth understanding,"
Because it cannot be understood/contained by the
mind.
I am awash in what seems most like mother's milk
Not actually remembering mother's milk
Something in me remembers this...
This is what I've always wanted
From everything I've ever done.
It was for this that I tamed fire, and made tools,
Built skyscrapers, dammed rivers, waged wars,
Climbed Mt Everest and walked on the moon.
This, only this, hidden Here, in the heart of it all.
This is being Home indeed.

Who We Are

Who we thought we were
Was of course hopelessly deficient.
It was only ever a thought
With no substantiality at all.

Without this inherent substantiality,
How could we ever feel secure?
How could we ever rest in peace
except for moments here and there?

Only by stepping outside of the world of thought
Can what is Real be seen.
What is Real, what is outside thought,
Is substantial beyond belief.
It is stable, it is the ever-present awareness that can,
yes can,
Observe thought coming and going,
heating and cooling,
striving and resting.

It is what everything rests on,
rises from and falls back into.
What is here before birth and after death.
What we really all Are.

Oceanography

Do some kinds of shellfish
live past the outgrowing of their shells?
Is there the possibility for them
Of easing out slowly
from the constraining tightness?

Such a beautiful shell
spiral bound, glistening with stars.

Is there a shellfish
that releases it's hold
and slides free
into the weightless wonder
of the moving tides,
Homeless in the immensity?

What wonder
To feel this easing in the human experience.

The unhooking from the moorings
The smooth glide out into the total vulnerability
with the willingness to be another's dinner
no more protection is needed.
There is nothing to do
But find the current
And go.

Chapter 4

Living from Awakeness in a World of Duality

The process of beginning to live from our new source of identity can feel effortless and free but may also sometimes feel very difficult. The layers of mental content in our psyches all seem to need to come to the surface (to be seen through) before we are free enough to simply live our lives as the new identity. The emotional foundations that lie underneath all of our mental content also need to rise into awareness in order to be embraced and included in the fullness of who we are. Ultimately the process can only be easeful, because we are not doing it, and our job is just to keep out of its way. Keeping out of the way of the process however goes against all of our habitual ways of being and so it can feel very uncomfortable and difficult.

I refer to this process as the "clean-up" because that is what it feels like in my life. It feels as though every bit of my old structure of making sense of the world is coming to the surface, becoming conscious and being seen for what it is: ideas. It is quite horrifying (though eventually amusing) to discover what the building blocks behind our thinking have been all these years. The beliefs and assumptions that lie deep within us often seem to be quite irrational and crazy. Though some of the layering can also be from more recent events, or maybe even from genetic or personality predispositions, much of what we have at our core was created from our thinking when we were very young and we didn't have enough savvy to realize that our ideas were ridiculous. An example of that would be a child's tendency to assume that everything is always their own fault. In my own young life, I seem to have believed that it was very important for my personal survival to appear to be as similar to those around me as possible and ideally, to be totally invisible. It was easy to see how this developed as a survival mechanism in the circumstances of my childhood but it was less easy to see the way it was still working underneath the more adult aspects of my personality and affecting my behaviors.

There are layers upon layers upon layers of this sort of content programmed into our minds, and each mind has both its own particular content and has its own unique relation to the emotions that are also stored inside. Though having layering seems to be universal, the content of it is unique to the person involved in that each person has structured their bundle of beliefs and assumptions around the core assumption of identity. Then there comes a point somewhere in the process where the clean-up moves from clearing the thought-based conditioning to the re-experiencing of the emotional states that preceded our cognitive functioning as children or that have been stored more recently through life events or traumas. These emotional layers feel palpably different and can be quite frightening because they are often feelings that we have spent a lot of energy avoiding. In this process everything will be coming up for inclusion and these painful feelings from so long ago are no exceptions. Their re-integration will be discussed further in the chapter called "Reclaiming Lost Parts of Ourselves".

A core belief is the one that informs each person about who they are and these are often based on the underlying emotions. What we experienced emotionally as young babies before our cognitive faculties developed can often be experienced simply as who we are because mind is not yet creating separation with its thinking. Getting to these core beliefs and emotions can happen at any time in the process, because working through the layering is not really linear and time-bound in the way that our mind would think it is. Often we can begin with the most basic level, with the realization that our old familiar ideas of who we are, are not really who we are at all. This realization might then begin the whole rest of the clean-up. Sometimes we can't really get at this core piece fully until we've cleared enough other layers out of the way first, and then we get to see it. Everyone is different. It's as if everybody is locked up with a different combination lock, and they need just the right combination particular to them, in order to get free. Life itself provides the combination, if we just don't interfere too much with the natural process.

I'm calling this clean-up a process, not because it necessarily has to take time, but because of the way I experienced it. Ultimately it doesn't have to follow any linear pattern or need to take time, but my down-to-earth experience is that the mind-made self does manage to obstruct full embodiment quite a lot at first, and then less over time. Eventually the personality structure seems to have a kind of transparency about it. It remains present, doing its thing, being helpful when it is needed, getting things done that need doing, and so forth, but over time we have a different relationship with it. It gets sidelined, and it doesn't have the solidity that it had before. It can make a lot of noise about some hot-button being pushed in its emotional body, for instance, but the noise is no longer central to the sense of self. The fact that noise is now happening is no longer a big deal. Who cares anyway? Is the essential Self affected in any way by the fact that there is mental noise one minute and none the next? No. Our true nature remains stable and unchanged, even if it may appear to be obscured or accessible at different moments.

As an example, I personally find that there are certain environments where it feels comfortable to be able to write a book like this, and other environments where the flow of words is not accessible. Similarly, there are also certain social environments that seem compatible with being fully present and others that seem to reduce me to being only able to access my mind-made self. So, in writing or in socializing, when the personality appears to become more solid and impenetrable, there is an opportunity for me to see through the mechanics of that. The layers of content which make those ideas seem true come to the surface and are able to be seen for what they are. I begin with the evident reality that I need a quiet environment to write this book. If the environment doesn't meet the specifications that the personality thinks are necessary, then no writing happens. If I push myself to write, I may well end up writing something that just reflects mind doing its thing. Additional tools to make the environment "right" then might be tried, such as lighting a candle or shutting the world out in some way. Mind can be very good at being helpful with all its ideas about how to manipulate the environment, but an essential part of this which mind doesn't "get" is that it actually doesn't matter whether those manipulations are successful or not. What mind misses is that presence is just as much 100% there in either set of circumstances. The specifications that I set up for successful writing are just arbitrary personality preferences that don't really need to be met in order for writing to occur (beyond real requirements like needing a writing implement, of course). The preferences that I mean are my ideas about what is needed to write, such as an uncluttered environment or a lack of noise. These ideas are then looked into and it is noticed that they are based on deeper level assumptions about my relationship with the world I live in.

The exploration of this material can be done on our own as seen above using direct inquiry, with the help of a skillful friend or with a professional. My way has been mostly through direct inquiry. The underlying assumptions that were revealed through looking into the need for quiet for my writing were about the need to control my world in order to survive. This was based on my seeing the world as a dangerous place that needs to be defended against. None of that turned out to be true. The preference for quiet remains but it is no longer an absolute requirement for writing.

Do we actually need to live in rarified spiritual environments in order to be good spiritual people? Do we need to only work in certain kinds of jobs, or have certain kinds of spouses or families? Look into it for yourself but, for me, the answer that has come out of this investigation is no. The essential breakthrough that is the culmination of what we call the spiritual life is to realize that what we are is already 100% with us and available, no matter what the circumstances that we are living in. From that knowing, personality still has its preferences, but it lightens up about having to get things entirely its way all the time. The mind-made self is finding its place in a very different configuration about how life works. As it finds that place, it finds that its job is much easier and much more doable than it ever was when it was trying to control things all the time. Now mind can just rest when it is not being useful doing the kinds of things that it really is good at.

As our awakening process unfolds, we find ourselves able to stay aware of the opportunities that come to us through our uncomfortable moments, and to welcome with honesty and openness all that life sends our way. The dualities of good and bad, spiritual and non-spiritual, black and white, high and low, open or shut, all are still visible. They keep giving richness and texture to the world we experience, but we are less affected by their changeable nature because our attention is more and more on that which does not change. In seeing the world in this way and letting what we see penetrate us fully, the opposites are found to contain each other, and then even the preferences soften. We find ourselves to be the one that contains both sides of all of the dualities, the one where they meet and find peace with each other.

Unmitigated Surrender

The "I" who hoped
When it heard about enlightenment
Had no idea.
Wanting to hold the ocean
In a cup
It thought it would possess This
As a personal asset
Earned through right thinking.
Instead it is blissfully unemployed
Tongue tied and inconsequential
In a world it never dreamed of.
What is Here wants expressing
And cannot be expressed.
So one writes,
Hopelessly lost
And staggered
At 3 AM
Amongst the radiance of simple things
And the incredible full/empty grandeur
Of being Here
In This, as This.

Chapter 5

Always and Already Awake

Strange as it may seem, one of the most common barriers to actually living an awakened life is not being able to accept the possibility that we are already awake. To convince us that we are not awake, mind uses as evidence that part of us that is human, fallible and imperfect. You might have been told a thousand times that everyone is already fully enlightened but it isn't a useful statement if your day-to-day experience is that of total involvement with the imperfect human parts of ourselves, without input from beyond it. It is just a matter of where our attention is being placed. It is possible for our human-beingness and our true nature or presence to exist wonderfully well together, enriching each other through their closeness. It is through the power of our attention that we experience one or the other or both. Just because we are fallible human beings does not mean we are not awake. We fulfill a special and amazing role as we let who we are embrace and include both and become a connection between the two. This could be called bridging heaven and earth.

Upon deep inquiry, we may notice that the deciding thought which lets us know that we cannot possibly be awake is generated by and in the mind itself. Mind is totally unable to see anything outside of itself. If mind's processes were to stop suddenly, it would be a very different world that we would experience. There would be a complete absence of separation, comparison, judgment, criticism/self-criticism, evaluation, and measuring. Can you imagine being without all those things and then asking the question of whether or not you are awake? Without those functions, the question no longer even makes any sense.

Our true nature that exists already, behind and before all the mind's activities, lives in another world quite different from the world that the mind has created through comparison and judgment and all of its dualistic thinking. A foundational idea in that mind-created world is the one that tells you that you are separate from everyone and everything else. This we accept as more true than the spiritual teachings telling us about oneness, because mind keeps collecting evidence to support its conclusions about our separateness. We experience a world where the outer forms of things appear very different one from another and people appear as obviously separate from one another. These forms interact and collide in ways that bolster the idea that they all are totally separate things. Meanwhile, behind this display of difference lies a reality of oneness that mind filters out because it is incapable of seeing it due to its limited viewpoint based on its dualistic thinking.

Mind is a miraculous and amazing tool, but it has a distinct limitation. It can't see beyond itself! What it can do for us is recognize its own limitations, and when it reaches those edges, it can relax rather than mobilize to protect against the possible "horrors" of what is unknown, what is beyond itself. Mind can easily become frightened by the unknown and begin to cause a great deal of stress because it does not trust anything outside itself and wants to stay in control rather than be insecure. Mind tends to take very seriously its task of protecting the insecure and vulnerable personal self's identity. Whatever is outside of the mental structures is the unknown and can't be controlled or manipulated by the mind, so it appears initially to be dangerous. We can however notice the thought mechanisms through which the fear is being generated and in that way we naturally begin to separate out real dangers from mind-generated fears of the unknown. As we pay less heed to mind-generated fears, we don't lose our natural responses such as stepping out of the way of an oncoming bus or taking our hand away from a burning hot surface. All of those body-preservation responses are still in place. They are not generated by mind's activity but are instinctive non-logical functions, and thus still can function perfectly.

By seeing through our mind-generated fears, what is naturally being left behind is the role mind has played in thinking that it is in charge of the survival of the separate organism—a role that it couldn't actually fulfill anyway. It was a role that was stressful to it

56

because it couldn't ever control the unpredictable things that happen in life, no matter how much insurance might be purchased or how much financial planning might be employed. Not that insurance or financial planning are bad ideas. We are just looking into whether it is mind that is in charge of keeping us safe as separate individuals. Can mind instead be free to buy insurance or do financial planning (or not), depending on a sense of knowing what to do that is coming from something beyond itself? This possible way of functioning relieves mind of the tasks that it can't actually do anyway, and relegates it to doing the tasks that it actually is able to accomplish. It can be a great relief.

When this shift is made, our identity that has all along been lying behind the virtual reality that mind has created is able to shine through. The question of whether or not we are awake has changed. The key word in the question is now the pronoun, rather than the usual focus on the activity or state being asked about. Who exactly is it that is asking if we are awake? If it is the mind-made self who is asking, then the answer will always have to be no, we are not awake. But if we stop insisting on that bundle of ideas being who we are, and it is our true nature asking if we are awake, then the answer is obviously yes.

A rather silly analogy regarding the already awake nature of who we are that has been helpful to me is that of a fried egg, with its white underneath and the yolk on top. If we consider the white as our awakened nature and the yolk as our mind-made self, we can get an interesting view of the relationship between the two.

In the case of the configuration of someone prior to awakening, we would have a yolk that is essentially as big as the white, covering it over so that the white is hardly visible. The white is no less present behind the yolk, but simply is not visible except maybe a tiny bit here and there around the edges. We can then liken awakening to a naturally generated process of shrinking the size of the yolk, making the white more and more visible at the periphery until the yolk is contained as a small but extremely useful circle within the much larger background of the white. Throughout the process the white is unchanged and stable as an unmoving background. After the process of shrinking the mind-made self into a smaller area, the unchanging background now has the space to be visible. It can now move and express the inherent freedom and Love that are what it always and already had been all along.

Who is Enlightened?

Am I enlightened?
The question is odd...
Who is asking it?
If the one who is asking
Is the separate person,
The isolated entity.
A subject surrounded by objects
Then no.
This one is not enlightened.
And has no hope for becoming so
Ever.
If the One who is asking
Is the One who can't quite
Be put into words,
The One who is aware
Of the rising and the falling of thought
And never moved by it.
Then yes,
That One is enlightened,
Always has been, and always will be
No matter what mental barriers are ever put up
To hide it's eternal presence.
This One has no need to ask.
This One does not measure and compare.
It is only the mind that needs to know.
So in answering the questioner,
It always must be no.
While outside the question
Reality sings yes
In the heart of All.

Chapter 6

Letting Life Live

The way we move from our identification with our mind-made selves can sometimes feel like an upward movement out of life. We are rising above our attachments, our assumptions and interpretations, and moving up and out of suffering and out of vulnerability to the changing circumstances which seemed to constrict our lives. Once this "up and out" part of the journey is made, there comes another part which could be called "down and in". We have realized who we are; we have touched the possibility of living from this new source of energy and life force. Now we must take the other half of the journey which is bringing that energy back into the details of our down-to-earth lives.

This is where our true nature can begin to interact with the world, and to offer itself to the world through us, as us. In this process we can't know how that is going to happen. One of the essential elements of our being able to bring our realization down into our human lives is a willingness to live and move without knowing the outcome, without knowing why to do things, sometimes without even knowing how. One of the universal characteristics of mind is the tendency to want to know ahead of time or to think it knows already. Mind likes to imagine that it knows what is going on, who is to blame for things, what the explanation is for things, and so on. But these are only its ideas about the world and they all get to be seen through. Over time we realize that most of what the mind has put forward as reality has been based on ideas that actually don't have anything real to back them up. To say this is not to discount the existence of some basic laws of nature that mind relates to, but just to emphasize the majority of thinking which is unnecessarily added onto that.

Seeing the mind's tendency to pretend to know when it is not really able to can be very uncomfortable, but allowing ourselves to see this makes us able to welcome a new way of living. We begin to function without knowing in the old way. We now have access to something else, a kind of flow that we enter into that has a wisdom of its own. This wisdom has not previously been accessible to the thinking mind most of the time. Often it has been used in extreme or emergency situations only. In order to live in this natural state of flow, there needs to be a willingness in each moment to not buy into mind's ideas about what is going on, what an action is going to lead to, why, and all of that. The awareness that mind is not really being helpful with all its ideas leaves open the possibility of living without limiting life by thinking we know it all ahead of time. This in no way discounts the value of education, training and skill-building in our lives. These can be valuable tools while living in the flow. It is clear that if we were facing heart surgery, we would want to choose a surgeon who had the most developed skills in the particular area that we need. This is not contradictory but would simply be obvious in that situation. Also, building our personal organization skills does not need to be contradictory to our ability to release ourselves into life's current. Such skills can interfere certainly if they are used in an agenda for mental control but may also be used in service of the natural flow of life moving itself along through us.

As we suspend or ignore our erroneous ideas that we ever really knew what was going on at all, we enter into the natural movement of life already happening, just as it happens, and simply leading wherever it leads. This may sound passive to the mind, but it actually is an incredibly creative way to live because one notices after a while that in each moment there is the most amazing expanse of possibilities for what can happen.

In my life, this was taught to me using the analogy of taking a walk. I walked generally in the mornings before going to work. Through holding the walking as an analogy for living in general, I became able to relax the mind's ideas about how long the walk was going to be, and where it was going to go, where I was going to end up and when. Then the walk would open up in a wonderful way and what could happen on the walk then would suddenly expand into the infinite array of possibilities that were actually already there. I could actually walk in any direction! I could walk and not stop until I reached the ocean! Such unusual options were not happening however, just being noticed. Normal options were also equally there. The difference was that I would be moving from freedom rather than from a mental idea about having to go to work to earn a living, from my physical limitations or anything else. The amazing array of possibilities would remain open, and in my freedom I surprisingly ended up going to work just as easily as before. Even within the seeming limitation of being on time for work, somehow each walk would be quite different from the day before, with an equally wide-open feeling of spaciousness and possibility. Like life, without mind's constrictions being listened to, each moment of the walk (and of life) could involve a change of direction or not. And each change of direction (or not) then would lead to a different set of experiences as the flow progressed.

It always seemed like a miracle when I took a walk in this way and still ended up back at my house without "making it happen" and without being late for work. There seems to be an incredible freedom that we step into when we let go of control of the details of our everyday lives (of which going for a walk is just one example). Life takes care of us and takes care of the details of our everyday lives in surprisingly effective ways. I guess it shouldn't be surprising. After all, that same force is already taking care of our beating hearts and balancing our endocrine system and a lot of more complicated functions than whether we show up for work on time. Evidently it can handle all of it. It is just a matter of our relaxing or ignoring the interfering mental processes enough to let life take over the steering wheel of our proverbial car, and drive itself.

Then the mental processes that are truly helpful to us in the practical details of living can take their appropriate places in our toolbox for living.

One of the biggest blocks to allowing this natural flow to occur in our lives is our tendency to hold up ideas about how life should be and then strain ourselves with trying to make our life look like those mental pictures. This can be a tremendous source of suffering because we often think that if life doesn't conform to our ideas of how it should be, then something is wrong. Many of us, myself included, have inserted into our psychology at very young ages the idea that we must set goals for ourselves about how life is supposed to turn out and then strive to make our lives turn out that way. Not that there is any problem with having goals, but the idea that there is somewhere to arrive at in the future that will provide us with happiness and fulfillment is a setup for unhappiness because we never actually get to the future. It's always up ahead. We are free to set a goal to be a millionaire and then may achieve it, but the problem is that the underlying emotional goal is whatever we thought that being a millionaire would bring us—safety, security, love or maybe freedom. This underlying emotional goal, whatever it is, will not be truly satisfied by simply changing our outer circumstances and the satisfaction that mind thought it would provide will be elusive.

Life seems to be set up like this so that eventually, because of our discomfort, we look into the ideas themselves and see through the psychological mechanism of trying to make our life conform to mental pictures of how life should be as a life strategy.

Through relating to the actual world that we are already in rather than living by mental pictures of how things should be or should turn out, we find both happiness and fulfillment are already here. Anything new can then happen in the next moment and the next in a flow of rich vitality in motion. Life becomes fresh and alive.

Abandoning the idea that life is only supposed to contain the pleasant things and not the unpleasant ones, suddenly the suffering that the unpleasant things caused us is no longer affecting us in the same way. Any unpleasant feelings or experiences are no longer a sign of personal failure at controlling life properly for the right outcome. The unpleasant things in life are simply a part of life, just the other half of the pleasant things, causing them to be perceived as pleasant by contrast. There is still pain sometimes in life but any remaining mental suffering is having less and less impact on our overall well-being. It becomes possible to actually enjoy what was not at all enjoyable when mind was in charge of life, in the same way that we might enjoy a movie even though it makes us cry.

Once we have touched the way it feels to live in this flow, knowing also how it felt to live in a mind-based reality structure, we now have a contrast. Often people experience that they appear to pop in and out of the awakened state, being in the flow one day and abruptly taken out of it on the next, based on the circumstances of outer life. This does not, of course, indicate anything about any change in the availability of the awakened state. There is nowhere to which our awakeness can go. Mind simply has been allowed to cover over the awakeness again for a while through its noisemaking capabilities. Then it becomes an opportunity for us to see through what the interfering noise is all about. Some pattern of mind has come up for examination and we only need to see what is happening from outside of it, rather than to use the experience as evidence of a lack of awakeness and then to use it to re-identify with the insecure and insufficient mind-made self.

There becomes a certain art to staying astride the flowing current of life that is moving us. It can sometimes feel like walking a tightrope, with the constant possibility of losing our balance either one way or the other, towards either side of any duality. As we wobble on our own unique tightrope, we feel the contrast between the two ways of living. The fresh aliveness of our life as it expresses our inherent freedom is noticed and contrasted with the suffering and hopelessness of a mind-driven life. We feel patterns still arising for clearing and the balancing act of staying in the fresh alive state while those patterns are being met and seen through. We live who we really are in each moment by seeing clearly what the interferences to that are and by allowing life itself to move in and through us, as its own conclusion each moment, always fresh, always perfect, and always including those interferences.

Life energy now flows from the core of our being, no longer from the conditioned mind. The mind is useful for worldly things, and is a marvelous tool, but it is no longer our energy source. We now get out of bed in the morning because life gets out of bed rather than because we think we should or so that our bosses won't fire us. We have taken our hands off of life's steering wheel and let go. Will life therefore take us into living in a cardboard box and feeling cold and hungry? Mind wants to know this and is quite concerned. We seem to have to be willing to have all of mind's worst-case scenarios happen in order to get through this. Could this be what Jesus meant about the eye of the needle? Are we willing to say OK to whatever scares us and to trust life enough to let go? This becomes the big question. If we try to retain or regain control in some aspect of our lives then that aspect will become a point of focus so that it can also be cleared. We can try to retain control out of fear—we always have the freedom to choose that too—or we can let go and let life have its way with us. This can feel like a dramatic moment in our spiritual journey, but the humorous viewpoint is that once we let go, we then see how life had its way with us all along anyway, and we are only now admitting it.

A common control pattern involves a resistance to letting go of a low self-esteem state that prevents us from engaging in work in the world that is visible or significant. Many of us, myself included, have a tendency to function under a mind-based control mechanism that encourages us to be small and humble, keeping our heads down and not doing anything that might attract attention. Getting out from under those kinds of constrictions brings a release of life force and activity that is surprising. Life force that has been pent up for decades under such constrictions finds its way into unexpected channels through us. Life-long physical tiredness retreats as the constrictions clear themselves and new directions for the life energy open up. The change-point, of course, is the source of the energy. We are no longer depending on mind to motivate us. Mind has its reasons, (its fears and other conditioning) that make it uninterested in motivating us in utilizing our life energy fully. Instead we now begin to allow life itself to move through us, as us, and we naturally move with life's current. This is what has been called "effortless effort" that the Tao Te Ching [12] describes so wonderfully. The old mechanisms for achieving our personal ends by exerting effort were something that was completely mind-generated. Now we move from another source, the same source that causes the water to flow, and the earth to turn. We have not mastered it, it has taken us.

Section 3

After the Realization

"...whenever you feel negativity arising within you, whether caused by an external factor, a thought, or even nothing in particular that you are aware of, look on it as a voice saying 'Attention. Here and Now. Wake up.' Even the slightest irritation is significant and needs to be acknowledged and looked at; otherwise there will be a cumulative buildup of unobserved reactions."

Eckhart Tolle [13]

"When we start to suffer, it tells us something very valuable. It means that we are not seeing the truth, and we are not relating from the truth. It's a beautiful pointer...it never fails."

Adyashanti [14]

Chapter 7

Our Conditioning and How It Clears Itself

The way that our mind-made selves are put together is both universal and unique. Similarly the process of deconstruction of the rule of our mind-made selves over our everyday lives is both universal and unique. One might liken the deconstruction of the self to the unwinding of a ball of twine. All of our balls of twine are different, some are very different and some are quite similar, with knots in different places maybe, but they all may be unwound by finding the outer end of the string, and pulling it.

Although it may sound that way, it is not actually you the individual person who finds the end of the string and pulls it. We as individual people actually interfere with the pulling of the string, not assist with it, except by getting out of the way. Life itself wants this string to unwind. Mind is so insecure that it is always getting in the way, getting over-involved, trying to retain something for itself. One of the biggest things it can retain for itself is to hang onto the role of being in charge of and responsible for what is happening in your life.

Cleaning up the way that our conditioning interferes with our ability to perceive reality and living in a way that is a reflection of that reality, is happening in spite of us not because of us. Yes, there may be some amount of preparation that mind has been of assistance in making (such as reading spiritual books might be) but the essential process itself is not coming from mind. The essential process of clearing one's conditioning is coming from everyday life! There is a way of being in each moment that allows whatever is happening to support the process—a way of being that is open to what is there and not relying on mind for its interpretations, judgments and comparisons. Then the clearing of the conditioning is found to be coming from our response to what our spouse said about us, our problems at work, our lack of work, our health issues, and so forth. You might have thought that those were the things that were in your way, right? If only I didn't have those things bothering me, then I could live an enlightened life! But those exact things are the perfect unique prescription that life is giving you in this exact moment, giving you an up-close and personal look at some particular part of your conditioned nature, your mind-made self. Finding the truth of this for you, is finding the end of that ball of twine.

We find the end of the string when we gratefully acknowledge some pain-in-the-neck issue that we would really rather ignore or eliminate, so that we could get on with being peaceful and spiritual. The mind-made self maybe gets excited and says, "Oh good, now I know what to do! I will pick up the string and do something with it... pull it or something!" Right? This is just another play for control by the mind-made self. Get accustomed to these and learn to greet them with a smile of familiarity. That is just what mind does. It doesn't mean any harm by it; it's just what it is in the habit of doing to be "helpful". "Oh, you want to get enlightened, or find the kingdom of heaven? I'll help you with that", says mind, but mind really can't go there. It is out of the range of its capabilities. So when it tries to be helpful in this particular area, there is no need to pay it much attention. It's just irrelevantly doing its thing.

If we don't pay attention to the mind trying to help out where it can't and are welcoming to the pain-in-the-neck issue because we are grateful for the opportunity to see the content that it brings to awareness, then we have entered a magical new way of experiencing everyday life. Life is no longer against us and giving us a hard time, but life is actually supporting awakening with every little thing that happens (or doesn't happen). It doesn't matter anymore whether our mind-made selves are happy or comfortable with what is happening, because often the most disturbing incidents can be the most productive in terms of seeing through conditioned layers and awakening into clarity and freedom.

Not only are the circumstances of our lives a perfect setup for our conditioning to clear itself, but within that setup are layers upon layers of opportunity for it to do so. We do still have our free will however, which means that if we choose to not accept any given life situation in the way described above, we are always free to do so. We do habitually tend to keep resisting certain things for a while which causes us to repeat patterns, and we simply keep doing so until we are good and ready to stop. Life has provided us with this setup such that we are always able to choose whether or not we are ready to go forward at every step of the way, and are always able to say no.

Knowing that we will sometimes choose to resist what life has to offer us at any given time, the setup is offering us layers of opportunity to choose differently. At the surface, when something disturbing occurs, (when something pushes our buttons or makes us afraid) we then appear to have a choice. We can either accept the disturbing occurrence then and there as it is, get to know it and see through our thoughts around it, or we can believe our thoughts about it, resist it, mentally justify how it was the wrong thing to have happen and decide who is to blame and so forth. If this choice is not an obvious one in the moment, it will gradually become more obvious over time as we get more familiar with our own inner mental structures and patterns. We will catch these choice points more and more quickly. If a year ago it would have taken us a week of fuming to notice that we had a choice about how to respond to our boss's misbehaviors for example, now it might only take a few hours to see it. Eventually it may become instantaneous.

When we miss this initial level of opportunity to let things be as they are and we choose to resist what is, we then experience some suffering about it. The suffering might be mild or it may be very painful, but resistance of any sort does create some amount of suffering. Then another opportunity becomes available to us: we can accept the suffering as it is, and not resist it, or we can choose to go deeper into the suffering (isn't free will wonderful?) and blame ourselves for experiencing suffering and maybe even call ourselves bad names or spiritual failures. Then another opportunity to let that be becomes available. If we choose to resist at each level, we are adding to our layers of conditioning by interpreting our experience, imbuing it with meaning, and storing it for future reference within our mental structures. Alternatively, if we choose to let what is be as it is, then there is an opportunity for us to see the underlying mental mechanisms that support the suffering for what they are. This exploration, in my experience, includes the sometimes horrifying, sometimes laughter-provoking realization that these underlying ideas aren't even close to being true. In fact many aspects of our lives have been based on a foundation of ridiculously erroneous beliefs and assumptions!

If, in a particular area of our lives, we have continuously chosen to resist what is, we may have created painful repeating patterns in our lives. We keep trying to "fix" the recurring situation or ignore it entirely, but neither strategy ever totally works. Perhaps we have some addictive pattern that just won't quit and we keep repeating behaviors until we begin to wonder about our own sanity. This is the same opportunity to accept what is, as it is, but because of the historical choices that we have made, the resistance to seeing into it can be very entrenched and itself hard to see. Long-held traumas and childhood wounds can be some of the most difficult material to tolerate and allow to clear. These kinds of issues may need to be worked through relationally with someone who specializes in this work, or in the company of a skillful friend who can accompany you along the way. This of course is an individual decision that each person makes on their own, using their internal sense of knowing what to do in each moment. Allowing life to heal our deepest wounds is not work for the faint-hearted. It seems to require us to be willing to drop our defenses against life which means letting go of the props that we have used all our lives to keep away our existential fears and to keep us comfortable. If we are willing to face this level of conditioned content, we then find we are also able to open ourselves fully to what life gives us in our daily lives and let life unwind the string on our proverbial ball of twine and complete whatever we are ready to be finished with in each moment.

Chapter 8

Identity and Self-Centered Living

What I call basic conditioning is the collection of beliefs, ideas and assumptions that are the foundation of our thinking patterns and upon which most, if not all, of our thinking is based. This would usually, though not necessarily, be things that we put in place when we were very young. As children we make conclusions like how fundamentally unworthy we are, for instance, based on our pre-cognitive emotional experience and/or our interpretations of what happens to us in our early lives. If these same experiences were to occur to us now as adults, we could easily interpret them quite differently, but once these basic feelings and ideas are established as foundations of who we are, we tend to no longer question them and in most cases don't even know they are there.

These deeply held and often unconscious feelings and ideas affect how we experience our lives and our world, how we interpret everything that happens to us, and what actions we take as a response to our interpretations. If, for instance, as a child we believed that we were not an acceptable person or that there was something fundamentally wrong with us, this long-forgotten conclusion may still be affecting how we interpret the behavior of the people around us. Without realizing it, we may filter people's words and actions looking for confirmation of our lack of acceptability. We then may feel compelled to defend ourselves or to conceal ourselves from others, to keep others from seeing our unworthiness. We would be responding very differently if we were interpreting everything from a standpoint of being acceptable and loveable.

In this way most any of our child's survival strategies can unconsciously still actively be in use by us as adults. These are often strategies about how to control the world as best we can, to get good things to come to us and to keep bad things away. They are driven by fear. While their original intent was to help us survive, we become driven by these strategies into repetitive and self-centered behaviors. Although I speak generally here about our collective experience, the discovery of my own underlying survival strategies has been a fruitful part of my journey. I can now see how my childhood survival and control strategies have generated all the habituated behaviors that caused me to think about and respond to life in the way that I was when mind was running the show. I had been enacting these strategies whenever I went out in the world but they became more noticeable any time difficult or problematic events occurred and I reacted to them.

An example is that a survival strategy based on the assumption of basic inadequacy was causing me to unconsciously repeat self-effacing behaviors as a way to avoid criticism. The idea seemed to be that if I first presented myself as inadequate, others might be less likely to criticize me for being so. In this scenario, events in which criticism actually were leveled at me put me face-to-face with my own conditioning. When someone criticized me for something, (no matter what my immediate response was) I had an opportunity to sit with whether or not the inadequacy was true, not for the other person, but in reality, in my own deepest sense of things. In this way the underlying assumption of inadequacy was asking for attention, and seeking resolution in the truth. I can't tell this personal story without also saying that the joke has been that yes, the separate self is actually totally inadequate! When I stop playing games around pretending otherwise or fending it off, it is just no longer a problem.

Events which show us our strategies by causing us to react are blessings in that they reveal to us some element of our conditioning, but the way that they feel makes us automatically want to avoid them. This is where we need to look into whether we have prioritized awakening over being comfortable. If we have not, then we may not be willing to experience the uncomfortable revelations about how we have been operating up to this point. We always have the opportunity to say no to this process, although I notice for me that saying no seems to have the tendency to create repeating patterns in my life until such a time when I am ready to say yes.

There are layers upon layers of habituated behaviors. The sum total of all of it is the identity that we have created that can be called the mind-made self. Of course, reading this now, it might be easy to see that we have been making up this self or passively accepting what we have been told about ourselves as we go along, but when we are fused with this mind-made part of ourselves in a stressful situation, it is often hard to see clearly. When we are still even partially identified with this version of who we are, it can be very difficult to see the conditioned layers of ideas, assumptions and interpretations that flow from the central survival strategies and constitute the supposed identity. We are imbedded in it so fully that it can be difficult to get perspective. When we begin to realize that who we are is not this bundle of ideas, but something else entirely, this process naturally allows the layers to become visible to us in its own good time as we pay attention to it. We can also find ourselves in this same process without any radical identity shift or awakening experience but just through a natural human maturation process. In either case we begin to see not only our particular content, but also the whole movement of the deep conditioning clearing itself out in its own way, in its own timing. If we stand just a little bit away from identifying with it, this allows it to begin to clear itself.

In my particular situation, the first big layer that cleared itself happened when I saw my mind-made self and its behaviors clearly and realized just how self-centered my life had been up to that point. Bear in mind that I never had been a proud or competitive person but lived a quiet humble life thinking that was a good way to be. The realization was that absolutely everything that I had done in my first 48 years, even the humility, had been done from the perspective of being good or getting something good for me, and keeping away whatever was bad from me: generally looking after #1. It was all just basic me-first-ness either directly or indirectly. It felt horrible to realize this! My entire life had been so self-centered, even my quietness and sweetness had just been coming from self-protection strategies. If I was caught in a traffic jam, I had really only cared about whether I got the green light, not anyone else. My relationships, even with my children had been managed so that I could get something good for me (like their success), and keep away whatever was not wanted by me (such as not having them do well.)

This was horribly painful to realize but this basic self-centeredness is the cornerstone of the life that we lead when we are identified with this mind-made self. This insecure version of ourselves really can't live any other way and it is only by beginning to dis-identify with it that we can begin to see what it has been doing all along. Once we see a pattern that we have been playing out for years, it begins to lose its momentum. After that we can't just blindly keep replaying the pattern because it is glaringly visible. If we don't resist it, but just view it as impassively as possible, it slowly runs down and loses energy, as it is seen for what it is. Then we are on to the next layer, whatever that might be in our unique construction of ourselves.

As I experience it, the process takes care of itself, and the job of the separate self that wants to usurp the process, is to notice that tendency and relax out of the compulsion to try to take charge. Beyond that, it's just a matter of my not resisting being uncomfortable and not condemning myself for what I see. It helps to have a sense of humor when catching myself red-handed doing things that have been embarrassingly unconscious and self-serving. When awakening has been prioritized above comfort then not minding this stuff isn't so hard, even while I am squirming with discomfort and wondering when it might ever come to an end. Even when it feels like it might never end it can as easily provoke a belly laugh as an outbreak of tears. After all, without the unconscious self-centered layer of conditioning being in charge anymore, the difference between laughing and crying seems much less significant. The automatic judgment that it is better to laugh than to cry isn't central anymore. Without the self-concern of the old made-up identity, we are fine with crying and letting someone else do the laughing for right now. It has become all the same.

Revealing the content of this basic conditioning can sometimes feel very uncomfortable. The amount of discomfort experienced seems to me to be the same as the amount of resistance that we raise. Without resistance, it is a natural and very humbling experience through which we come to know ourselves in a deeply intimate way. This paves the way for a new ability to relate more intimately with all that has previously been seen to be separate from us.

Chapter 9

Conditioning in Relationships

Sooner or later in the clean-up process it becomes time to look at how our conditioning is affecting our relationships. The relationships that we think about first are the bonds that we have with the people that we love. But those are only one level of the entirety of relationship, which includes the way we interact with our whole world and all the things and beings in it. In all of our relationships we are likely to have had the tendency to be using the same self-centered survival strategy with which we also run the rest of our lives. When we identify with the mind-made self and all of its assumptions and interpretations, we end up using the world in general and all the people that we love to achieve our self-centered ends. We feel we have to control it all somehow, to be in control of our own life. To the mind-made self, all of the different kinds of relationships in our lives are just supports for those self-centered survival strategies, whether they are intimate love relationships, family bonds, a simple exchange with a store clerk or even how we relate to the chair we are sitting in and all of the objects around us. All of the variations on relationships become a reflection of our basic strategy for living.

It was a shock to me when I realized that all the relationships in my whole life had been self-centered and self-serving. I was devastated. It had not been obvious to me along the way because it had been done very subtly. There was an unintentional and subtle kind of manipulation that had been going on in all of my relationships. I had made all the people and things in my life into pawns on a big game board on which I was trying to win by making life turn out the right way. In order to be (or become) the "right" kind of person, I needed my parents, my children, my spouse, my friends, my surroundings to be "right" also, and so with all the best intentions in the world I set to work to mold all of it so that it agreed with my mind's idea about how it should be. This of course took the fresh, alive quality of life out of my experience, and life assumed the quality of struggle.

An example of this was how as a parent I wanted my children to get good grades in school. Not that my children getting good grades in school was a bad idea of course, but the implementation of that as an idea was a subtle manipulation of my children's lives, trying to make them conform to some idea that I had about who they should be. The difference between that and just being with them fully and giving them space to be whoever they really were may be subtle, but the two ways come from radically different paradigms for living, and have a very different feel to them. Children have built-in radar to detect such a difference. Within the range of what was possible for my children's authentic development, there was naturally the possibility that they might get good grades and be successful, but trying to force them into this outcome through manipulating them into being who I wanted them to be, or getting the grades that I wanted them to get, was never going to benefit any of us. It could only push us apart. While it is a part of the parenting role to encourage the development of values and conscience in our children so that they will not be likely to be out robbing banks, the effort to be controlling in relation to them, even in that way, defeats their natural inclination to be their authentic selves.

Does our personal separate identity have to manage our relationships in order to keep us safe? Or is this another irrational assumption that we have adopted from somewhere back in our own childhoods? The baseline assumption says that "I" am the separate self and "I" need to manage life in order to control it so that it turns out the way that "I" want it to turn out. From the patterns of difficulty that I see in the relationships in my own life, it seems fair to say that I have a tendency to bring the most immature aspects of my being to my intimate love relationships to try to work them out there. That often seems to mean relating from my mind-made version of myself no matter how aware I might otherwise be of my true nature. This is the source of the discomfort by my own observation. The discomfort seems to be generating from the unfulfilled needs of the child that remain unresolved in the most immature recesses of my humanness. This could be used as a wonderful opportunity to put to rest these kinds of longstanding issues except that when the most immature parts of me overwhelm the awakeness it is not at all easy to retain the ability on my own to step out of the mentally mediated reality that holds it all in place. I seem to need outer support to do that and generally look to the other person to support me in those moments. One thing that has happened for me is that the relationships themselves have been prioritized by me in the past as being more important than the resolution of the childhood neediness, or to put it another way, relationship was being used as a way to try to satisfy that neediness and to cover it over rather than as an opportunity to truly heal it. This is obviously a set-up for trouble if my priority is awakening.

Our already present awake nature doesn't handle or manage our relationships or anything else. Our awake nature is actually being served by our relationships in amazing ways. Our relationships bring into the light whatever interferences to the flow of life are still buried within us and are often fraught with our deepest issues. Following closely the content of what comes to the surface and inquiring into it deeply as we interact in relationships is a very powerful tool for moving into living fully what we truly already are. Our relationships are shining a light on whatever is arising for us, as a service to awakeness itself.

Although we will always choose someone for an intimate love relationship who is a fit for our own unresolved issues, the information that our relationships can bring to us in this way is particular to us, and doesn't really have a lot to do with the other person. It can be easier to see how this is true by looking into the patterns within the simplest of our relationships, the ones where we have the least history. Take for example the interchange we might have with our mailman or our neighbors. In such a simple relationship, we can begin to distinguish between the subtle manipulations involved in getting something that we want (through trying to make life conform to how we think it should be) and accepting the other person exactly as they already are without our mind-made overlays. We can begin to recognize a very different feel in the two ways of relating, or rather the two identities from which we relate: one mentally mediated through our ideas and one not. When we are ready, we can bring our insights into the more complex relations that we have with our family members or friends. It is a matter of watching closely what we are up to when we relate to others and of approaching what we see with openness to what is true. We need to be aware of when we relate through a screen of ideas and when we do not. A simple curiosity and a spirit of exploration are what are needed.

Although we often prioritize the importance of our more intimate human relationships over other things in our lives, we also can often sabotage those same intimate relationships by putting things like security first, ahead of truth and authenticity. There seems to be a prevalent pattern in our culture of using relationships as a place to hide, as a place to satisfy the mind-made self's craving for safety and security. If we can just find that "right" person, then we hope to be set for life and our personal agenda then becomes one of not rocking the boat. We then do our well-intentioned best to get our partner to conform to our ideas of what our relationship should look like. This agenda is reinforced if our partner is doing the same, and we may well end up as a caricature of ourselves and wonder why our lives are not satisfying. Seen from this perspective, one has to wonder if it might possibly be a good thing that our society has such a high divorce rate! If we are mired in our relationships, then life naturally does whatever it can to get us unstuck, and get us back to a way of living where we refer to our authentic core for direction as opposed to fulfilling the idea-based agendas of the mind that our society has given us.

Seen through the lens of life being a perfect setup for awakening, the difficulties that we have in our intimate relationships that lead to such a high divorce rate are simply signposts. They are alerting us to something that requires our attention in the process of having our conditioning made conscious and eventually cleared up. There can be a wonderful simplicity in just seeing what is there without allowing what is seen to be spun into additional layers of mental content. When layers of conditioning are simply and curiously seen as just what is, we find that the conditioning is no longer actively creating our life experience and instead it is now just transparent. This transparency combined with our willingness to look into how our conditioning is constructed then allows us to see who it is that we really are and who it is that we are with, without the meeting being colored by that content. This can be a tremendously awe-inspiring moment, although it also can feel crushing to realize what we have been missing for decades with our self-serving habits of mind.

Once this view of what life has been all along is seen, once the true nature of our surroundings becomes visible through the layers of conditioning, it can then feel like we are beginning life again. Now an entirely new kind of relationship with the world and our loved ones becomes possible. We relate not as someone separate with an agenda in the world, but as the world itself, interacting with itself, loving itself through having these individual natures. Each moment takes on the fresh alive feel of surprise as we discover every day what we are going to do and how we are going to live.

The awakeness that is already there in us accepts all people and all life situations exactly as they are and has no agenda to change them except as lightly held preferences for the overall well-being of ourselves and others, alongside an honest not-knowing of how to achieve that. As soon as we see something other than equanimity is going on, we can see it as the relationship's gift to us of revealing some interference to that awakeness, and we can work with it internally as such. When the internal work is being done, things change outwardly in remarkable and wonderful, though totally unpredictable ways.

From my own life experience, relationships give me access to a deep level of my own emotional core content that I wouldn't otherwise have. While this is the uncomfortable part of any relationship, it is also the richest. I do feel that I have, in the past, made the mistake of assuming that because the relationship is providing access that therefore the relationship also will be the place that the material is worked out. I feel that this is just not true. Although relationship does have the possibility of providing us a supportive environment where it is easier to work with the material, still we must work it through on our own internally. In the end relationship cannot give us what we are most deeply yearning for. We must give that to ourselves. When we are satisfied internally and our issues have come to resolution internally, then we will be able to enjoy our partner without the complications of our mental and emotional projections. All our loved ones are freed as we free ourselves.

I am in the process of learning to live that statement fully. Relationships are continuing to be a mystery that is unfolding in my life. It appears that it is often the case that living the fullness of our spiritual lives within our closest relationships is one of the latter pieces to resolve itself in the journey. It seems obvious that this is because letting relationships resolve into freedom involves meeting and embracing the deep existential and emotional roots that generated our whole mind-made self experience in the first place. For me this has required a willingness to knowingly enter into painful areas of myself that seem to resolve more slowly than other areas and to stay there until these things awaken also. It feels as if the pull to awaken is the only force strong enough to propel me through this process to its natural ending in freedom.

Relationship

Holding each person
as the perfect and amazing work
of mystery made manifest
is the source
of the joy of truly being
with the wonder of each other.

Accepting all imperfections
within this greater perfection
and remembering the sacredness
of the mystery
that made each of us
just This way,
restores our ease,
awakens our delight.

No more
becoming someone separate
to act out a drama,
even a happy story.
Another way has appeared:
simply releasing any outcome,
of wanting, needing or getting anything.
A simple acceptance of what is Here
no more, no less, than just This.
Now there is nothing
but the wondrous and total satisfaction
of being complete.

Poem to Spring Love

Buds breaking, in motion
Towards the lushness of summer leaves
Through the quick celebration of flowering,
Life paints itself
With a delicate paintbrush
On the hills
In a thousand shades of green,
As I drive between them
In awe and gratitude.
Yesterday my wonder was full and complete
In Love with the world;
Overflowing...
Today is new again; remade through your touch.
There is the ecstatic arch of my spine
Alive in the bedrock
Deep under the swell of the hills
Rising and falling, riding the greater breath.
Your touch is in the penetration of air
into unfurling leaf.
Your eyes awaken remembered green
Touching the hills with springtime.
Your voice celebrates in birdsong,
The joy of being alive.
Thus do you enrich the ground of this day.
I split like a seed.
The roots stretch into the mysterious dark for
nourishment,
Feeding the unfurling bud
In it's journey toward the sun.

Chapter 10

Conditioning Around Spirituality

Surprisingly, one of the areas most heavily mined with traps and cul-de-sacs in this process is the area of spirituality. We come into the spiritual arena usually hoping to gain something for the improvement of our mind-made selves, innocently thinking that spirituality or religion is a good way to be rescued from the discomforts of the ordinary world. If we don't get caught in the cul-de-sac of thinking that there is one right religion and that everybody else is wrong, then we may be ready to look more deeply into the core of what it means to live a spiritual life. The common culturally approved practice of adopting someone else's ready-made belief system is a way of finding the support of spiritual community. While spiritual community can be very comforting, if we are asked to accept particular beliefs in order to belong, then our long term healthiness may depend on our ability to look into those beliefs deeply and inquire into what really is true for ourselves.

I notice that the expectation I started into spirituality and religion with was backwards. I expected that I would be improved by my spiritual pursuits and in the end discovered that the one who wanted improvement was an illusion. By following the inquiry into our spiritual beliefs and identity to its' natural end, and not being stopped by the desire for comfort along the way, we find that this process has really been about discovering who we always were before we adopted our illusory and sometimes quite spiritually attired identity. Along the way we have taken on the trappings of our spiritual traditions and worn them as part of our mind-made identities.

Spiritual life is not essentially about living in a right way, accepting particular beliefs, or practicing the right rituals or methods. It goes much deeper than that. If we follow it far enough, it undercuts the identity with which we began the spiritual search, and reveals to us that the old ideas of identity were not based on anything real. Meanwhile the truth of who we really are (and always have been) is constantly available behind the noise of the search and all the commotion of our effort to perfect our spiritual discipline and practice. It just quietly waits for us to notice it. This does not justify rejecting our spiritual practices. This simply challenges us to stay with the central inquiry in our exploration of spirituality and to not be distracted by our egoic efforts to perfect our separate mind-made selves through the various beliefs, costumes, forms and rituals that spiritual life can take. There is another possibility too besides using all these religious trappings in the agenda of the ego. All of them can also be a way to access the loving divine energy that is also available and which can nourish our human hearts through our practices directly.

Religions, traditions and spiritual paths can so easily be institutionalized avoidance techniques which the mind-made self uses to maintain dominance. They also hold the potential to be used as ladders with which to ascend out of that dominance. There are many choice-points along the way in anyone's relationship with a spiritual path. The underlying factor that makes all the difference is what one's priorities are. It is what we really want most that dictates how we make our choices along the way, for example in deciding between things like comfort and security or continuing to penetrate into the heart of our spiritual life. We may not be sure, if someone asks us, what it is we really want, but the decisions that we are already making can show us where our true priorities lie. For instance, if we have entered into being a spiritual seeker hoping to find the security that was lacking in our lives, then the path will naturally lead to a choice-point where we are asked to choose between security and continuing to inquire into what is true. At that point we can go either way. If security is more important to us, then we will stay there and not be interested in risking that seeming security by continuing on.

When we begin on the spiritual path, the separate, mind-made self is in charge and wants to be told what to do to be a spiritual person: how to behave and what to practice. We adopt a set of behaviors and practices to help the separate self know it's being spiritual. At this point the exercises, rituals, meditations, prayers and so on that come with a religion or tradition can be very useful. Such things are a benefit for that whole stage of development where we know abstractly about something greater than our own separate little life, but are still divided from actually experiencing it everyday. At any stage, however, the beliefs that come with our religions or traditions can become a potential trap. It is so helpful to see beliefs at any stage as something that we have decided to have or not have. We do not want to be trapped in the illusion that any belief is an actual reflection of some objective reality. A belief is a mental construct. If we stay loose in our relationship to our beliefs and hold them lightly and only as long as they seem useful, we can then be ready to let them go if and when they are outgrown. We are also free at any time to use them fully as conduits into a non-abstracted and vital reality that they are signposts pointing to. To use beliefs in this way can yield deep unifying encounters with the divine in our lives. These again need to be held lightly and not incorporated into a system of mental constructs that takes the life out of them by freezing them into something static and immovable.

One of the biggest traps within the spiritual life is that of becoming attached to one set of beliefs, accepting those beliefs as reality and stopping the inquiry into what is true for you in each moment. This acceptance will have the effect of making shallow and flat a life that might otherwise be vital and vibrant. Any time we hold our ideas as reality we are reducing life from its full aliveness and, instead, we are freezing life into a mental picture of itself that makes us unable to experience its vitality. Our core ideas, if we believe they are true, filter and constrict our perception and cause us to see a world that is a poor and distorted copy of what exists outside of our mental frameworks about it.

If we are able to see our structure of beliefs for what it really is and not allow it to constrict our view of the world, we are then free to use our spiritual path or religion as a helpful structure for supporting the process of ascension into freedom, wholeness and unity. The many different ways, traditions and religions can then simply reflect the personal and cultural differences that humanity exhibits. We honor these differences and do not need to find fault though we are free to see areas that may be in need of completion or openness. In the same way that the deconstruction of our conditioning is unique according to the content involved, each of the different religions or traditions is unique to a particular type of person or to a particular culture. We see how there is a way for every one of us and tools for every one of us, according to who we have been in the rich uniqueness of our human stories.

Chapter 11

Mind as Servant

Once we have discovered our freedom from mind's dictates which are either based on the past or on some projected future, we may feel as if we have entered a new world. In this new world, mind has a very different function than it had before. Previously mind was working very hard to try to stay in control and to help the organism survive, and who we really were was being dominated and used by it for its purposes. A different possibility has now arisen.

The human mind can be likened to a computer that creates kind of a virtual reality experience of life for the individual body-mind, based on the content of its programming. It is also a storage device that stores up and regurgitates what is put into it. The trouble comes when we locate ourselves in the center of the programmed-in content and then use it to relate to our world. Often we aren't even aware of what the programming is and yet we are still being affected by its existence under the surface. Some of the programmed content has been stored from earlier times when it may have been useful. Other content may appear to be utter rubbish. Even though it may appear to be causing a lot of trouble, the overall substance of the mind's programming has been an effective mechanism for ensuring our survival up to this point.

One of mind's useful functions has been that it has censored the input it receives according to its programming, to keep us from being overwhelmed. Through its efforts to do this however, it has narrowed our perception in ways that we aren't aware of, and it has created our particular individual experience of life by doing so. The way that we experience our lives is dependent on the conditioning that our minds are using to decide what is important or unimportant in our environment. Unfortunately, what mind, with its survival-oriented programming, thinks is important is anything that might be threatening. What it considers irrelevant is that which is eternally at peace. No wonder our lives can feel so fraught with stress and tension. Mind is always on the lookout for danger, while something like beauty can so easily be considered irrelevant in its world of separateness and survival.

While generally well disguised with more civilized intellectual activities, this survival-oriented programming still underlies our other mental structures and creates a life filled with fear and all of the things that come from fear, such as the seeking of survival, approval and control. As we begin to shift from total identification with our mind-made self, this programming can begin to be seen for what it is while we relax and see it as currently irrelevant noise. This re-sets the way mind filters what we experience as we go through our days. With this reset, we find that the world that we live in is quite different than the world that we previously seemed to be living in. The difference is in the way that our perception is working, the way it is filtering the relevant from the irrelevant and interpreting incoming information. Life has become simpler. For example, if our spouse had ignored us while we were having breakfast in the morning, we might have interpreted that action according to what we know of him or her from the past, made assumptions and then assigned meaning based on those assumptions. We might even take some action, perhaps go on the attack, based on our assigned meaning, and gotten an opposing reaction in return. If we relax from taking our assumptions and interpretations as truth, our spouses' preoccupation at the breakfast table is allowed to be simply what it is. The mind may still be running its programs, making its habitual noises, but this is no longer central within awareness. It clearly isn't relevant. It is as if those thoughts are happening off to the side somewhere, and they still may be noisy, but they are being seen through as a process separate from our direct perception of the world around us. How we respond to our spouses' behavior now will be unpredictable, but it will be filled with openness rather than with preconceived ideas about what is happening.

Until now, mind has held a powerful central place in our inner world, helping us survive, and in order to do so it has dominated us. Since we are now becoming aware of our true identity, this is the time for mind to instead begin to be used by us. In this role, it turns out to be a most miraculous servant. Mind becomes more and more available as a tool that functions within the awakened presence and the powerful nature of mind as a tool can feel shocking. The mind is now freed of a lot of the content, less hooked to whatever is left, and feels much more spacious, while still retaining its practical capabilities. It still knows how to be useful, and still is interested in being useful, though its role has shifted dramatically. Mind's usefulness now is in assisting the newly recognized real Self to do things, and often to take care of the basic necessities of life. It also still has a creative side, with a wonderful ability to bring thought into reality in the physical world. Thought can respond to images of what is possible and then know what steps to take to bring that image into the physical reality. Thought followed by action can build houses and plant gardens. Thought can translate things into words that make a difference in people's lives.

The pictures that we hold in our minds now seem to have a stronger ability to attract the reality that they are picturing. However, this particular and miraculous gift of mind can also be a distraction along our way. Mind can lure us back into old ways of functioning through ideas about manifesting money and other things that we might have always wanted as an ego-based entity. It is always advisable to check on ourselves at each moment when we begin to realize this power of the mind surfacing, and be sure that we have not fooled ourselves back into believing that fulfillment and happiness is at some future point when some new thing is "manifested".

When mind stops interfering enough so that we are able to feel the incredible vitality of life, there is a constant sense of completeness, of enough-ness, that is never available through having our desires or preferences fulfilled. When mind wanders into being overly interested in itself, a creeping sense of lack arises and with it, an inclination to fix the lack through doing or getting something. At this point it is the same whether we fix the lack through using normal methods of earning money or by being manipulative, or to fix the lack through clever use of the creative power of the mind. Neither will satisfy. Both are fear-based.

This is not to discount the amazing powers of the mind, nor to say that they must not be used. Why would we be given such a gift if not to use it? In fact, we do use it all the time unintentionally. To use it intentionally is what is a concern, because who is it that is in control of its use? Who is being intentional? This can be a very grey area, where it is difficult for us to see what identity we are functioning as: the mind-made self or our authentic Self. The true Self is at peace and does not experience lack or anything that needs fixing so the feeling is quite different. It only seems to wield the powers of the mind with a very simple playfulness and with a delight in life and itself. If in our experience there is still fear, lack or strategizing involved in our use of mind, no matter how subtle, it is best to minimize intentional use of the powers of the mind as a way to address those motivations.

In the end, these powers are not ours, but belong to life itself. As separate and fear-based individuals, we have been collectively misusing these powers and this is what has gotten us into the messy circumstances that define our world situation. It is exciting to discover the power of the human mind but it is something to be very careful with. We need to make sure that the discovery of our mind's powers does not become a new support for living a life based on the personal survival and improvement of the mind-made self.

Section 4

Troubleshooting the Living of This

*"The interconnectedness of all things: Buddhists have
always known it, and physicists now confirm it.
Nothing that happens is an isolated event; it only
appears to be. The more we judge and label it, the
more we isolate it. The wholeness of life becomes
fragmented through our thinking. Yet the totality of life
has brought this event about. It is part of the web of
interconnectedness that is the cosmos."*

Eckhart Tolle [15]

*"What do you really want after all?
To win, to pick the sweetest fruit on the tree?
Or to rest from the endless succession
of temporal moments
and the promises that they never keep?*

*What do you really want?
To take or be taken?
To find the Great Pearl of liberation
or to be consumed by it?"*

Adyashanti [16]

Chapter 12

Believing Your Thoughts

There is a wide-spread idea that once we have progressed along the spiritual path far enough, that there will simply be no more rubbish emanating from the thinking mind. While this may be the experience of others, it is not my experience so far. My own experience has been that the mind keeps on making a lot of commotion, but the relationship to the noise has changed. There is spaciousness now around the noise that mind is making, including an awareness of the silence within which the noise occurs. It has somehow become a noise that is occurring outside of the core identity, not within it.

There is an acceptance of the noise as just mind doing what mind does: thinking. The thoughts are not assumed to have any merit whatsoever. Behind the scenes, there is an old habituated assumption that our thinking does have merit and does reflect reality, but this begins to be seen as just another thought. When the mind starts making noise about something, there is a sweet tolerance now. It is trying to help, but its limitations to actually being able to help are obvious. There is a gradual realization that what mind is coming up with, outside of practical matters, is as likely to be totally "out to lunch" as to have one iota of truth in it! The ramifications are beyond belief!

Yet, until our conditioning has finished the work of clearing itself out, we will at least temporarily have a tendency to want to believe what the mind is telling us and enact that belief to some extent in our outer lives. Falling for what the mind is telling us is actually one of our most prominent signposts, telling us that some new layer of conditioning is ready to be seen for what it is. Having been caught in this way by the mind is a signal to pay attention to what is happening in that moment. What is happening, for example if we catch ourselves believing our mind's interpretations about a friend, is that it is distorting our ability to see the friend as they truly are. Noticing these thought patterns, we can also see that we do not have to make negative judgments either about our friend or about ourselves for having been temporarily caught by mind's interpretations. Getting caught in this particular trap is a signpost from beyond the separate self that here is the next layer of content to have a good look at. Here is the area that we are now ready to start seeing into, so that we can become more aware of how it is that we are constructing our daily experience with our habitual thinking patterns, faulty assumptions or random interpretations.

It's not a thrill to begin to see this kind of material about how we've lived our lives up until now, but this is the process that leads to freedom. My own approach has been just to see it fully, to get to the bottom of what it's about as best I can, to not judge myself for it, and to move on. Knowing what I really want (awakening above comfort) makes it so that it no longer matters if seeing this makes me uncomfortable or even horrified. Whether we are horrified or not is of no consequence. It is only the separate mind-constructed self that cares. We are now looking from outside of that separate self, and the one who is now looking at those thoughts is completely unaffected by them, and totally at rest.

Touching True Ocean

Mind,
amplifying its roar;
its gargantuan effort to preserve
or better yet, enhance somehow
its caricature of Self.
comprised of layers and layers
of stories, coverings, costumes, pretendings.

Masks of ideas
spread over the surface
of the deepest ocean
making it appear shallow
with paintings of fish and seaweed
scattered appropriately to mimic
what "should" be here.

Where underneath,
sometimes completely obscured from view
a glint of vivid blue-green...
an upsurge of joy and aliveness, as
a flick of fin glistens
and disappears into the deepest mystery
of what lies beyond and behind the surface.
The living world calls us to other-worldly color,
bright with the vibrancy
of what is truly Here.

Chapter 13

Referencing Other People for Reality

One of the universal experiences that we all have gone through is that of being born knowing nothing, and making our way through childhood and adolescence to adulthood. This process is fraught with all sorts of difficulties, no matter how good or bad our parents were, just because of the human condition. The world and all of its goings-on takes a lot of getting used to! Some of us may conclude that the world is entirely insane and make accommodations based on that. But probably the larger proportion of us turn against ourselves as children, thinking that the world must be OK and that therefore there is something wrong with us. This was my own experience, and by looking deeply into my own childhood it looks as if the emotion of feeling flawed may have preceded my ideas about it. In any case, once cognition was active, I used what evidence I had at the time, made interpretations with a child's lack of perspective and concluded that it was true that I was fundamentally flawed in some way. The world can't be insane - it must be me!

From a fundamental childhood feeling such as this came a survival mechanism of self-abandonment and betrayal that has chased me into adulthood. As an adult I found this feeling of being fundamentally flawed at the base of a variety of behaviors that limited my ability to fully live the realization of my true nature. In hindsight I am able to see that this underlying feeling of being flawed temporarily broke the inner connection between the child's felt identity and the fullness of who I really was. This was the beginning of a pattern of self-abandonment that can still reassert itself and affect my interactions with the world at large and with the people that I love if not held in conscious awareness. It is at the root of why I may suddenly turn away from my true identity and instead fall into old limiting ways of behaving.

As children, when we look around and see the craziness of people and the beauty of the world, we naturally and innocently know that this is beyond our capacity to understand. This at least was my own experience. Something appears to be going on that is beyond us, and we just don't have the resources to figure it out or to know what to do with or about it. In my case, having assumed that the problem was occurring because of my own inadequacy, then I naturally begin to look for clues outside of myself that might illuminate the situation. I look especially to my parents and then to whomever else is around, for clues as to what is going on and how to handle the situation that life has given me. When I looked around, everyone else seemed to be OK with things, knowing all about life and acting like it was all fine and comprehensible and how it was supposed to be. This led me into the habit of looking to others for clues that would help to heal my inherent ignorance about life and teach me how to cope and how to live.

As I began to habitually look to other people for information about how to act, how to be, how to survive, I used my sensitivity to the people around me to always be scanning for new clues. But as my thinking matured and I developed more perspective, I began to notice that other people really didn't know what was going on either. I had assumed as a child that they knew something I did not know, but all the time they were working with the same basic material that I was using in trying to make sense of life. They were only doing the best they could with it all, having taken their imprints and limitations from their own parents. They were just putting a good face on things.

What a freedom it has been in my own life to realize that it no longer makes any sense to look to other people for some right version of reality, or some "how to live" information to clue me in about life. What a freedom to stop being hyper-sensitive to everyone around me as a way of enacting this old survival strategy and at the same time to be able stay open to people and to learning from other people's experiences of life. I had been trying to control my life experience by always looking for clues from others about how to be instead of just being who I was and accepting life as being the way it is. Now people can be enjoyed!

One of the things I notice as an adult is that typically people in our culture aren't very interested in or capable of meeting each other in a deep way, but are instead relating façade to façade. One of the reasons for this kind of surface-oriented relating, it seems to me, is that so many people are looking outward for information on how to be, and giving back according to that information (according to what others want to see or hear) rather than being willing to be authentically themselves. Without being aware of it, many of us have established from our early survival mechanisms our own versions of how to make it through various situations as best we can. We may copy the way of living that our parents modeled for us, adopting it unawares and in that way perpetuate through our families an interpersonal distancing habit and various defensive stances in our ways of meeting each other.

The pattern of looking outside ourselves for the answers in life can take many forms but if it remains active in us as adults it can hamper our ability to be in our relationships in a free way. Without the clearing of this kind of underlying tendency, we may feel free when we are by ourselves or in nature, but our relationships still may feel strangely complicated and problematic. Our human relationships may consist of a lot of subtle manipulations and pretenses because we still may be wanting to get something from other people that we have not yet given ourselves. We may still be looking for security or love or approval or any number of things. Whatever it is that we are looking for, we then will manipulate our behaviors to achieve that goal and we are no longer free to just be who we are.

Without bringing the fullness of who we are to our relationships, we don't really meet the fullness of anyone else either. It's as if a door is closed within us, not allowing a true meeting with others until we are able to open it from inside, to accept ourselves fully as we are, and then simply and naturally let that live in the world.

Chapter 14

Reclaiming Lost Parts of Ourselves

As the story of our personal lives has unfolded, we have done what seemed necessary along the way to survive and be good and successful people, but sometimes it can feel as though we have abandoned parts of ourselves in the process. Without reclaiming those parts that have been pushed away, left behind or covered over, we find great difficulty in fully embodying the spiritual truths that we have realized. It is as if we know the truth, but some indefinable force holds us in our old reality, not allowing us to fully experience that truth while in the midst of everyday life.

No one else can ever say for us what is really going on. This is something that only we can know from the inside out as we move through the particular and unique content out of which our seeming prison is constructed. Yet there may be some universally true commonalities among all of our experiences so that we may benefit from one another's stories.

As discussed earlier, in our childhoods we are often in situations in our families, schools and society in general where the best thing our immature little psyches can come up with for a plan is an abandonment of Self in favor of putting on the masks that our situation seems to require. For some reason it isn't common knowledge in a lot of families that children need encouragement that who they already are is acceptable and lovable. Instead we are taught that what is important is to construct the right façade to cover over our inherently unacceptable nature. People don't generally think about it that way of course. We are encouraged to be good kids, to please parents or teachers, to do the "right" thing, and generally conform to the requirements of our situations. Kids don't think about who it is that is conforming. Their self-reflective capabilities are not yet well developed. I didn't think about it, I know that much. So the authentic Self that I was born with was partially lost in the shuffle to conform and survive.

As we move through a lifetime of experiences and relax out of more and more of our conditioning, we naturally and lovingly move to reclaim who we inherently were before we built our facades. In my case, a major clue that this process needed work was that I had a strange and complicated relationship with food and eating. The complications were obviously involving something other than just nourishing my physical body, and seemed instead to be about a deeper hunger. It turned out that eating was for me a fabulous barometer, letting me know if at any time I was neglecting vital parts of my aliveness. There was a healthy and natural hunger in me for the things that really mattered in life, like love, connection and presence that would turn itself into an unnatural appetite for food if it could find no other way to be satisfied. Different people will have different signals from their unmet emotional needs (based on what was picked up from parents and others) and a list of those would be the same as making a list of all of our society's favorite addictions.

I realized through observation that my emotional eating or any addictive behaviors were trying to treat the unmet childhood needs in ways that would never truly satisfy them. This led me to look even more deeply into what the roots of those behaviors were. That self-observation became a way to access core emotions in my being that seemed to have begun in that pre-verbal childhood period where there was no cognitive differentiation being made between myself and the distressing emotions, and the pain of them was experienced as the same as who I was. My ability to access those old emotions again was supported at that time by circumstances in my life which triggered those emotions back to life/back into awareness. These events could easily have been seen to be the wrong things to have happen to me if it were not for the context that they appeared within and the obvious opportunity that the emotional access provided.

The intensity of my old childhood emotions needed to be endured off and on over a period of several months before I began to feel more in harmony with letting these parts back into my awareness. That length of time probably just reflects the resistance that I put up to welcoming these deeply held parts of myself that had been kept under the proverbial rug for over 50 years. Now as an adult, I was the observer, watching this process happening, still pained by the emotions but now having enough perspective to be able to welcome them back into the larger adult context of awakening. This larger context seemed to contain the feelings in a way that was not possible as a child. Besides creating resistance (and even occasional panic) mind also seemed to have the role of following and trying to understand what was happening enough to be able to communicate about it. This allowed it a role in serving this process rather than just obstructing it with its fears and its preference against feeling anything painful.

This experience brought me some very valuable earthy wisdom about remembering to stay firmly and consciously in my body as the awakening process moved through me, and especially in these areas where pain is stored. The body can serve as a wonderful barometer telling us about our emotional state when the information can't get through in other ways. There is a wonderful koan-like paradox around the need to stay with the body throughout the identity change from constructed self to real Self. Staying in close touch with my own body, with the energy in my body, turned out to be an important piece, and that information came from having an eating "problem", not from either the mind or from the inherent wisdom. This illustrates again how we are actually served by what we have previously considered as things that were in the way of our spiritual advancement.

It's not enough to just know who we are if we are refusing to allow parts of ourselves to be included in this vision of oneness and beauty. If we have abandoned some part of ourselves through the process of surviving whatever has happened in our lives, we now seem to naturally be able to reintegrate that part back into the fullness of who we are if we are just willing to allow those parts to come to awareness. This can be painful and it can feel very threatening. Yet our true Self is just waiting for an opportunity to embrace and include whatever early fears generated our childhood abandonment of our whole selves. To be willing to allow the opening of this painful material is a practical, gutsy way to allow the Love that connects and contains all existence to also be brought into our own mental, physical and emotional bodies. As we stop keeping parts of ourselves hidden and separate from the loving fullness of who we really are, the separation we experience from the world magically begins to disappear. Reclaiming lost parts of ourselves can also be said to simply be loving ourselves, all of ourselves, even and especially the parts that we don't want to include and have kept in isolation. All are welcome in the awakeness, and all are needed for us to be able to fully live that awakeness in our everyday lives. Without this deep inclusion of the rejected pieces of ourselves, our love is limited to only certain circumstances and moments. Without re-integrating the lost parts of ourselves into the whole, we cannot totally experience our oneness with our world and everything in it. We seem to be like a hologram: unity within, unity without.

For me at least, there is also a trap in this area. I encountered a strong pull when dealing with the discomfort of this kind of content to seek the safety of using mind to actively engage with it in well-meaning analytical processes intended to work through the material in order to become free of it. This might show up as a fear-generated mental analysis of my physical health symptoms for instance. Although such things do bring to light interesting and helpful information, in my case it became obvious that the analysis would never quite finish with any issue that it intended to solve. Things would perhaps slightly improve for a while based on the new information but then something else would happen, and the analysis would just deepen into unending complexity. This kind of analysis was eventually realized to be one more mental ploy for control over life. Everyone must obviously decide for themselves when their ideas can provide them with understanding that is helpful to their process and when those ideas become an exercise of mental control mechanisms which do not allow space for a deeper knowing.

What I also found in myself was a tendency to make the re-integration of lost parts of myself into personal projects that the mind-made self undertook for self-improvement and control over experience. This always entailed thinking of myself as a flawed individual who needed some kind of fixing (either physically, emotionally or psychologically). This assumption always seemed to be hidden behind the well-intentioned willfulness of the little me retaining control by deciding to clean up its own act. The truth of the matter of course, while all this was going on, was that the one doing the fixing was the only problem. It was strengthening its pretense of being me through it's well-intentioned but misguided attempts to fix itself. The reality was that this version of myself never did actually exist except in my mind, and that the one who really was here didn't need fixing at all. This is not to discount any psychological or medical processes that may be available to us for healing, but just to point out how it is possible to use them in ways that hinder awakening.

When we see that we are reclaiming lost parts of ourselves it gives us a new way of understanding what might have otherwise been interpreted as a loss of awakening. If we get up in the morning one day and find ourselves in some kind of suffering, we might previously have thought that we had somehow lost our awakening, because we seem to have fallen back into some old pain or old habitual pattern. But with this new perspective of bringing all of the lost parts of ourselves home, we can hold our "bad" day in quite another light. It's not that we lose our awakeness ever, even just a little! Where could it go? It's that our awakeness has to penetrate and embrace all of these lost parts of ourselves, in order for us to be able to fully embody it. In that process, all those parts must come into consciousness to be seen through for what they are. Nothing can be left out. Our moments of seeming backsliding are not that at all! They are moments of opportunity to meet some old part of ourselves that we have pushed away in the past, and welcome it into the Love that is who we are.

There are two typically religious beliefs that seem to also be relevant to reclaiming lost parts of ourselves. Those are the ideas of forgiveness and of loving one's enemies. If one takes away the religious connotations from these ideas, they can be noticed to be relevant to the topic because they are about accepting or letting in some part of life that we have historically held separate. These include people and happenings that our mind thinks shouldn't be that way and that we judge as wrong, bad, weak, or anything else. Such people and occurrences have been showing up in our life as signposts pointing out some aspect of our greater selves that we do not yet embrace and include within the circle of our identity. These are parts of humanity that we would prefer to leave outside that circle as something that we must resist or fight against however we can.

Take Hitler for instance. He is always a good example of an aspect of our collective being that we would prefer not to acknowledge! To forgive Hitler for what he did would mean to accept the source of his actions in our own hearts and to meet it with Love there. This is not easy to swallow, especially for those of us with years invested in trying so very hard to be the good people in life, while judging others as being the bad ones. To relax this defensive positioning and to see our world without judgment and let it be enough just as it is, is an affront to our deepest worries about doing right vs. doing wrong. We are afraid that if we open our hearts enough to let in Hitler that there could only be a bloodbath of bad behaviors that would ensue in our own lives. We would have no constraints on our behaviors anymore. We could be committing the next murder in the park, the next genocide of the innocents -- where would it stop? And yet Hitler stands before us as an outgrowth of a part of ourselves that desperately needs to be included in the circle of our love and acceptance, and thereby released.

Terrorists threaten our lifestyles with violence and destruction and we are afraid. Meanwhile we are taught in our religions to forgive, to turn our other cheek and to love our enemies. This can be seen to be a call to acceptance of yet another part of ourselves that we have held separate in fear. This is truly the only way. We cannot hold these parts of ourselves (the Hitlers, the terrorists, or the driver who cut us off in traffic) separate forever either. They come to us through the circumstances of our world, asking for a response, asking for our awareness, asking for resolution.

We have proved to ourselves over and over that one cannot overcome hatred with hatred, have we not? There is only one direction left to go with this. Looking deeply into the issue, what new response can we make to the situation that our world presents to us? What is it that can meet anger, injustice, torture and genocide with peace, harmony and love? Or should we say, who is it? Who is it that is holding it all, within whose peace all this is occurring? This is who we are. The way that we react to the appalling aspects of our nature has to do with our basic fear. This fear (and the defenses around it) is a narrow gate through which we must pass in order to find ourselves at one with life.

Chapter 15

Adopting the Whole Process into Our Separate Identity

At any point along the way, it is possible for the mind-constructed version of who we are to make attempts to contain the whole awakening process within its own limited story. Instead of waking up out of our constructed mind-made self, that mind-made self seeks to usurp the process and make it into something that is happening within its own limited perspectives, seeking to enhance and strengthen its own sense of itself.

The mind, until it stops, is going to keep making noise along the lines that it has always done. In my own experience, all the usual rubbish that mind has been feeding us all of our life is going to still be there. No longer do we believe all the things it is telling us but it just keeps trying for a long time, maybe forever. For me, it initially worked very hard, making a lot of noise, trying to reduce the awakening to being an experience that happened once in the story of the separate person of Alice. It wanted so badly to contain the experience within what it knew, and make it understandable within the mental structures of the limited version of the self.

Is it obvious what this would do to one's inner world if one allowed the mind to usurp our awakening in this way? One would quickly be moved from living in the incredible aliveness of the real world to the mind's pretend version of awakening! Fortunately for me, it was clear what mind was up to, and I was able to take actions such as finding companionship with others who had not themselves buckled under this mental pressure, as a way to support the awakening and to put into perspective the pressure from the mind. Essentially it seems that the one ingredient in this that matters the most is the ability to stand aside from the mental processes and keep seeing them for what they are, instead of being pulled into believing them and accepting what they are presenting as true. It comes down to not believing our thoughts.

Mind keeps tossing out the bait, and if we do not stay aware, we find ourselves biting onto some mental hook or another, that then draws us back into the limitation of living in a mentally constructed identity and world. Being hooked in this way need not be permanent though, unless we believe it to be permanent or believe that it signifies something negative about us. In fact, each trip back into that mind-constructed world can simply be seen as an opportunity to learn about what hooks us. Each time that we find ourselves hooked into being reactive to a situation or person we are being invited by life to explore that piece of our mental framework. The situation has simply given us access to it.

Based on the obvious situation of everyone having different mental constructs and conditionings, each individual's process undoubtedly will have unique characteristics. For me, besides generally wanting to contain the awakening process within the personal perspective, there was a secondary agenda that ego tried to use to usurp the process. It wanted to glamorize of the process itself! Instead of letting the process just be what it was, the separate self started being entertained by the drama of the process and thought it was doing something right. If ego can't get through the front door, it tries the back door! This back door approach is a way we draw off of the energy from the awakening process and cycle it back to feed the mind-made self by trying to make the awakening into dramatic and inspiring spiritual entertainment for itself. This is just the flip side of thinking that one is so flawed that awakening couldn't possibly be happening. This is, "Wow, awakening is happening and it's wonderful, so therefore I (the personal separate self) must be getting bigger and better!" A symptom of this cul-de-sac happening in one's life is that awakening has become very interesting and dramatic, keeping the mind endlessly entertained. Each new chapter or dramatic interlude leads to the next in a continuous progression. The way out is just simply catching it, seeing it for what it is and relaxing into the simplicity of whatever is really happening as opposed to what we think about it.

Chapter 16

Choosing Truth over Comfort

If there was one factor most responsible for the continued awakening of those who seek the truth, it would have to be that of consistently choosing to seek truth over the comforts that appear to be available along the way. Each stage of development that we move through has its own kind of comforts inherent in it and we may be tempted to settle for those comforts instead of some far-away-sounding spiritual destination that mind isn't even sure exists. Also, many of the relationships that our fellow human beings will offer us along the way will be based on seeking some kind of safety, some way of teaming up to protect against the threatening outside world. So many of us, myself included, have fallen into marriage vows that seem to hold us to a status quo that is a major compromise with what we know to be a life based on the truth. In numerous ways society encourages us to compromise our highest potentials or intentions and to settle for something much more mediocre and less threatening. Without the awareness that we are deciding between truth and comfort, it is very easy to simply choose comfort and not realize until later what we have turned away from.

By what means can we avoid these kinds of diversions? There is, of course, not a method, but only a cultivating of an awareness of our deepest intentions and a willingness to look inside ourselves to find our own most authentic responses in each moment. We each have an internal navigation system that can guide us as we move through life, though it can often become buried under the noise of our thoughts and ideas. If there was anything that might be called a method to deal with how to make the little decisions in life without compromising truth for comfort, it would be to unearth this internal navigation system and be true to it and to ourselves in all of the little day-to-day decisions that come along, as well as the occasional major decisions.

Resonance is a word that is very useful in unearthing our internal navigation system. There is a feeling of resonance when we move one way which we may not feel in moving another way. A different word for the same thing might be "flow", to borrow from Mihaly Csikszentmihalyi [17] and others who have written excellent books on the topic. Different words have been used by various authors and they have found diverse applications for it in many areas from sports to business. The basic idea is that we can all discover an optimal way of moving through life and that when we are in this flow, we are actually being supported and moved by capabilities and energy levels that were previously quite beyond us. In this state of flow, the movements in our lives are felt to be coming from the core of our being, not from our conditioned mind. In this flow it is no longer a matter of us against the world, but us as the world, flowing forward in a continuous movement with ease and naturalness.

To follow the resonance, flow or as Joseph Campbell [18] phrased it, "to follow our bliss", is what leads us to a doorway into a new world. This lies underneath all of the mental noise that overlays it and often totally obscures it. Giving attention to what else is available besides our mental evaluations regarding a decision we may need to make, we find that there is another level of input underneath. It is input that doesn't always speak in words but that nevertheless moves us in a way that retains the highest level of integrity with our true Self. It is usually mind that is louder, giving analysis and evaluation, and choosing various kinds of comforts and delights to satisfy our senses, our bodies or our ideas. This advice from mind is not always bad advice. Being comfortable does not have to conflict with our deepest integrity at all! We are not required to be uncomfortable. But without the voice of our resonance alongside mind's advice, behind it, below it, above it, without this rather instinctive kind of knowing as a part of our decisions, we are liable to spend a lot of time exploring multiple cul-de-sacs along the way.

One particular type of comfort which may easily side-track us is the comfort of conforming to one's surroundings. There is something very non-conformist about awakening in the midst of a society that is, for the most part, operating from a totally different, totally mind-based paradigm. There is a natural attraction to seek out people whose mental constructs are most like ours, so that we feel more comfortable with our personalities, values, and such. We can relax more if the people in our surroundings agree with us. For instance we can imagine feeling the difference when attending a party with a lot of people who agree with us politically compared to one with people who disagree. One set of social surroundings supports our mental frameworks; the other will find them challenged at every turn. In the latter we have to work hard to maintain our set beliefs, arguing against opposing beliefs just in order to maintain our individuality, dignity and our sense of self.

When we regularly seek out this kind of comfort in conformity, we find that our mental frameworks become more and more solidified over time. They are supported by our surroundings and we are more inclined to believe that they are actually true, and not to question them. This comfort seeking has then caused us to close down to the kind of open inquiry that leads us to the truth of what is really going on. The solidification of our supposedly right ideas which occurs when we live in an atmosphere of conformity also leads us, in the larger frame of world politics, onto the battlefield, where entrenched belief systems justify all sorts of violence and hatred. If we can simply be aware of our human tendency to find comfort by surrounding ourselves with people who have similar belief systems to our own, and see how doing so can side-track the integrity of our exploration into life, then this tendency will no longer have the power to derail us or send us off into battle with our supposed enemies.

In religion we see the tendency towards comfort through conformity brought to the forefront in the spiritual community. When religions promote the adoption of a set belief system, mind can be very comforted by the company of the many other people who are doing the same. Mind draws strength out of a scenario where people have the same belief systems and therefore are supported in the idea of the inherent rightness of those beliefs and the wrongness of the beliefs of others. This strengthening of our belief systems constrains the open inquiry into what is really going on, through thinking that we have all the answers.

When we notice ourselves thinking that we have all the answers, or demanding of ourselves that we have them, it is a good time to look deeply into what part of ourselves that is. My own experience? Thinking I know something is so often just my mind trying to be in charge of something that is beyond it—trying to reduce things into what is understandable within its own black and white dualistic thinking. All mind can do is try to win the next battle, crush the next enemy, or be crushed. Any final resolution endlessly evades it, because each time an enemy is vanquished, a new challenge appears. Each time we might be vanquished by an enemy (meaning any outside forces, including poverty, bad luck or ill health) we are renewed in our resolve to fight on for our cause against all odds. This endless struggle is just mind doing what minds do. It is not who we are.

Yet all this rises up out of the oneness of who we truly are, and when we let it all go, what we truly are is what's left, still here, still at peace, still loving itself and the world. What could be more comfortable? Mind leads us astray in search of comfort but we learn to turn away from the comfort it promises in order to discover something much more stable than mind could possibly imagine.

Chapter 17

Mind's Basic Control Strategy

Behind all the mind's different tricks and traps lies a basic strategy of working to maintain control over whatever is going on and trying to make life conform to some idea of what it thinks life should look like. Underneath all the patterns that are unique to our personal makeup, there is one universal underlying emotion: fear. Fear is what we find when we look deeply into the psychology that binds us to our pasts, to our suffering and to our outmoded ways of thinking and behaving. We all have fears. Fear is what can constrict us to our sense of separate self, even when we have seen beyond it and discovered who we really are. Fear is mind's core weapon in its strategy for keeping control over our life. When all else fails, out will come mind's big guns: our fears, and we may find ourselves quaking from one mind-made terror or another, afraid to proceed, afraid to go back, just plain afraid. When our fears are allowed to influence us in the large or small decisions that shape our lives, we become capable of all the terrible actions that dominate the attention of our news media.

Nothing but stepping into and through our fears will resolve our discomfort and give us entry into a world free of fear. The discomfort of this is the fire that we must pass through on our way to resolution, on our way to leaving behind the whole world we have constructed out of our fears. Avoiding this fire will only perpetuate the discomfort.

Who knows what the fears might be about? We probably have at least a vague sense of the content of our own particular configuration, of what our deepest darkest terror is, that lies under all the civilizing influences of our personality. We may remember from the dim memory of childhood what it is that we are essentially afraid of but in a way it doesn't matter what it is. What matters is that we are ready to meet our fear; that we are willing to be plunged into whatever the worst of it is because we know our freedom to be more important to us than our being comfortable. Once this willingness is present in us, we may meet our fears with great drama or with relative ease depending on the content of our personality structure and the depth of the fear itself.

At the outside edge of our awareness there seems to yawn some unnamable threat that signifies the worst possible thing that could ever happen or be. This is the fear itself, which by its simple existence constrains our behaviors within the confines of what is considered normal for our society, gender, family and time. The equivalent of this in the biology of the body is the natural instinctive survival response as withdrawing one's hand from a hot surface, rather than being burned. This fear is the mind's equivalent response, conditioned into our brains to help us survive in a dangerous world.

In modern times though, this fear has developed into a constraint on the whole way we live our lives, keeping us within the bounds of what our conditioning as a whole considers normal and appropriate. In practical terms this may be very useful. It may keep us from laughing at funerals or from neglecting to pay our bills. We benefit from constraining our behaviors to fit the norms of our culture, our times and our well-considered ideas of what it is to be a good person. Yet this function of the mind also works to keep us trapped within these constraints past the point of usefulness. Mind misguidedly tries to keep us safe by throwing up a wall of fear to stop us from leaving behind these constraints, even when it becomes appropriate to do so. This fear is based solely on mind's alarming ideas about what life outside its control might be like, just because it doesn't know. Mind cannot conceive of safety coming from a source other than its own workings. To the separate mind-made self, passing through this stage can feel like stepping off a cliff because mind cannot see where support or safety will come from other than itself. Stepping off of such a cliff can take a lot of courage and we may delay for a long time this meeting of our fears.

Whenever the time is right for us, we will begin facing our fears because they will come up. Part of our readiness is that through awakening we develop our connection with our true nature and because of it we feel held by a more solid and unmoving safety than mind could ever provide us. We are connected to a stable background within which we can see fears rising and falling and which is unchanged by those movements of mind. With this connection stabilizing us, we are not so much affected by facing our fears as we would have been previously. We are still afraid, but it is OK with us to be afraid. We hold it in the context of an unmoving background and are no longer engulfed by it, so it has become tolerable. Fear has become just one more part of the clearing of our conditioning.

The specifics of how the mind clothes the fear will vary according to an individual's experiences in life and can often be traced back to early childhood experiences that set into motion basic patterns of behavior throughout that lifetime. This raw material can be very uncomfortable to face up to, but at its core it is all only fear of one sort or another. If we can notice also that the fear is well-meaning, intended to protect us and help us survive, the intensity can become much more bearable. It is a defense that has played a vital role in helping the human species survive to this point in its evolution.

In the end it is the fear itself that must be addressed, beyond what is being feared. Whatever ideas and mental pictures are frightening us; they are just the effects of fear, not its cause. The cause is a sweet protectiveness based on not yet fully knowing that there is now quite another possibility for this organism, for this life: a new source of a different kind of safety. Through identifying with who we truly are, we are now in touch with a stability which can easily contain the arising of all of our fears and remain totally unperturbed by them.

Woman of the Dawn

Awake at daybreak
One foot in the dark world
Of unconscious deadening patterns
Of need and striving for what is not here,
As if for a cure, a completion,
That never comes.
Always remaining out of reach
In a future that never arrives.

If I lean, out of balance, towards this,
I live in constant danger of falling
Even into death as the un-fulfillment of all hopes and
dreams.
Yet as I stand upright in this
Seeing the tendency to lean and not leaning...

Holding the tendency to lean
Together with the tendency to love without bounds
Like a balancing scale
One in each hand outstretched
And place my feet on the firm ground of this moment
And this moment, and this one also...

Then the light of the world dawns
Through and within the darkness.
I stand as woman of the dawn.
The sun in one hand, shadow in the other.
Through me the world awakens again
In the exquisite celebration of color and birdsong.
Another day begins.

Chapter 18

Nowhere to Stand

We have looked at what scares us most in life and been willing to meet it with love and inclusion. We have lived through reuniting with all the things that we had pushed away when they came back to us and we included them also in the whole of ourselves. We are being watchful in every self-centered moment and in every reactionary mode. We are loving this that we are, being at one with this that we are, through it all.

Having passed through the narrow gate guarded by mind and its fears, we now have gained entry into a world which is totally outside of any thought we might ever have had about it. It is a world so without thought-based foundations of any kind, that we feel as if we are free-floating in a sea of raw possibility with no edges. All the constraints are gone, yet we do not seem to be a danger to anyone because we are no longer separated from our fellow human beings in the way that we were in our mind-created reality. We are totally alone and at the same time totally at one with the whole sea we are afloat in, including everything and everyone there. But something very fundamental has disappeared and the enormity of the loss may dawn on us slowly or all at once. Mind had provided a foundation on which we could stand in order to know how to live and who to be, and that foundation no longer is there. Actually it never existed in the first place.

We have entered a world where we now see "what is" without the screen of mind interfering. Thinking of it ahead of time, this may have sounded like a good thing, but when it does occur it is simply what it is: not good, not bad, just itself. Somehow even as the vibrancy of life, sound, and color has been enhanced, there is also a strange neutrality about everything. There is an awareness of a total involvement with everything and a lack of involvement at the same time that is difficult to describe. It is a different world than we inhabited previously, though to say it that way is twisting it, because we are what has changed.

To live in this seemingly new world (the world as it more plainly is) is to live without the old structures for placing oneself. It is also living without having thought-based pre-set kinds of relations with the world that inform us about how to live and behave. Yet somehow each moment continues to arrive with the plausible and ordinary simplicity of just being here. Movement continues to occur without our usual old entanglement in thinking our way into it. We move freely in this world, unfettered by the old structures by which we previously measured ourselves and our surroundings and with which we made judgments based on those measurements. We now have nowhere to stand, no security in the old way, but at the same time there is something else that might also be called security—an unchanging steadiness that is palpable behind all of the movement. We notice a background from which our movement arises and into which it disappears. Against the steadiness of that backdrop, we still have all the same freedom of movement and choice that we had when we were identified with our mind-made selves. In fact our freedom feels enhanced as we leave behind our old limited viewpoints and move freely in a wider spectrum of possibility for what we might do or say, or what could happen at any moment.

With our free will intact, there is a constant opportunity to choose to stay in this groundless place or to seemingly leave it by reinstituting the mind's control strategies (where we pretend that we know things and function as if they were true). A favorite example is to pretend that we are not yet awake based on some observation of ourselves that seems to prove it to us. Accepting this as true and behaving accordingly seems to return us quickly to a world constrained by history and habit. "Seems" is the important word here, because actually we are all living in this unconstrained world of total freedom already and there is nowhere it can go. All we can do is to turn away from it and reinstitute the mind-made prisons that appear to confine us.

Staying in this groundless place means being willing to let the mind not know the answers that it wants to know and to just let that be as it is. It means facing squarely the reality that has actually been true all along which is that mind has no idea what is going to happen five minutes from now, let alone a week or a year from now, and to keep functioning anyway. It feels like a huge insecurity from the mind's viewpoint but the deeper reality of it is a feeling of freedom. If we don't know, then anything can happen, including things that we never thought of. This includes things beyond our confined ideas about good outcomes, things that are better than we could have imagined! Without the mind's ideas around good and bad, even the things that we previously considered were bad or wrong can be seen in their fullness, just as they are, without that judgment.

An auto accident can, for instance, still injure or kill people, but without the mental structures that say that it is the wrong thing, it is experienced simply as it is, a major life experience that while very painful is also potentially a change point: a turning of the courses of all the lives involved in new directions. If we don't judge occurrences as being the wrong thing because they do not jive with our mental pictures of how life is supposed to be and therefore call them bad, then that occurrence is open to being a lot else: possibilities beyond the reach of our logical thought. We don't know for example, if something that happens in the life of a passer-by because of the accident is a thing that will change the course of the world. We have to let go of knowing. We don't have the answers anymore. We just let it all be just what it is, and by some incredible miracle it all seems to come to flower in the sense of stimulating our collective awakening. Seemingly negative events and even extremely shocking occurrences can be used by awakening to help us break out of old habits and enter into whole new ways of relating to life. We lose our old way of placing ourselves (and everything else) in our world and in the process we regain access to something groundless but substantial that was there all along, serving us in every heartbeat and breath in our bodies and in every delicate balance in our ecosystems.

Section 5

Is There an End to the Process?

The simple answer is no, but having said that, it sounds as if I know something, which I don't. So perhaps to say more is helpful, who knows?

Chapter 19

Ending and Beginning, All at Once

It seems like a logical question to ask if there is an end point to this whole process, where you finally arrive at total peace and are completely finished with conditioning and reactivity and all that unpleasantness. The question, however, is itself coming from the mind-made identity. The reality is that both sides of the duality which the question assumes are true.

We were done before we started. Even in the state where the mind-made self was totally dominating our awareness, our Self was actually untouched by that. The reality of our already awake nature was present all along. What we thought about it was not what was really happening. What was really going on was that we already were at the goal that our separate self set itself up to achieve, while thinking that we were far from it. Right now we are all totally and fully enlightened, and totally living in the kingdom of Heaven, the kingdom of

Love. The thought that this is not so, is just another interference.

At the same time it is also true that we always retain these human-being suits during our lives in the world of form. These human-being suits always retain an aspect of fallibility and incompleteness, at least in my experience. It seems quite dangerous to assume otherwise. This danger is illustrated by the corruption that seems to befall people who take (or are given) a lot of power, particularly noting those individuals who are in guru type roles. There seems to be something inherent in being put on a pedestal above the life of common humanity that tends to bring on an abuse of that power, be it through unethical sexual exploits, money, Rolls-Royces, or whatever. It is therefore important not to allow others (or our own thoughts) to convince us that we are somehow above anyone in any way. We have found the reality of our unity with everyone; we have not become better or more enlightened than others.

Indeed it is our completeness that allows us to contain that human frailty and fallibility and not to hold ourselves separate from anything. This is not to say that we will choose to behave unethically just because we know we contain that which is unethical. This does not follow at all, strange as it may sound. To embrace and include the dark, incomplete and fallible aspects of what it is to be human somehow allows us to contain them without having to act them out. It is only through resisting or disowning these aspects of being human that they can find a foothold within us and demand that we compulsively act on them as a way of their finding resolution.

There follows a favorite poem by Rumi, which expresses so wonderfully the welcome that we are now able to give all aspects of our humanness, as if now, in our completeness, we are a Guest House, where every sort of person can now find rest.

Guest House

This being human is a guest house.
Every morning a new arrival.
A joy, a depression, a meanness,
some momentary awareness comes
as an unexpected visitor.
Welcome and entertain them all!
Even if they are a crowd of sorrows,
who violently sweep your house
empty of its furniture,
still, treat each guest honorably.
He may be clearing you out
for some new delight.
The dark thought, the shame, the malice.
meet them at the door laughing and invite them in.
Be grateful for whatever comes.
because each has been sent
as a guide from beyond.

Rumi, "Guest House" [19]

Chapter 20

Completion and Incompletion
Enjoying Each Other

As we live in a way that welcomes our humanness and does not reject any part of who we are, there comes into our lives an enjoyment that permeates all of our activities as well as our quiet moments. No longer do we need to escape into meditation, prayer or the beauties of Mother Nature in order to feel the fullness of our true Self. The fullness is apparent in every little thing that is happening. We see a squirrel climbing a tree in the park, or we take out the trash or vacuum our home with the same wonder and enjoyment we previously may have only experienced momentarily in the most spectacular sunset.

What is even more surprising is that there comes to be an enjoyment even in our personal calamities and natural disasters. Painful events are still painful, but even the pain contains a quality of enjoyment. We can feel its opposite within it and experience the deep richness of life through it. We let the pain be there with us, as a natural part of the whole of what life is, and let it flower within us, deepening us into wholeness. In fact, everything seems to have a tendency to lean towards its own wholeness in our vicinity.

The places in life where we want something, need something, or are hurting because of something, are embraced within their fullness, as an essential part of it all. We are not so concerned whether the pain is our own or someone else's. It is all the same. We no longer find a benefit in having the bad things in life be happening to someone else, rather than to ourselves. There is nothing magnanimous about this. It just doesn't seem to matter in the old way.

From this lack of it mattering, comes an ability to enjoy all of it, just for being what it is, just for its being there, just for our being there experiencing it and not for any other reason. Previously we needed a reason. Previously we censored our experience, constantly deciding if we thought it was the right experience or not, comparing it to some ideal experience that we thought we were supposed to be having, and then struggling to make it conform. Now, without the busyness of those processes, we are able to see what is really there and what is there is perfect, even if it hurts us. We can't know that this moment's circumstances aren't exactly right in terms of the big picture which we can't fully see. No one ever did promise us life would be a rose garden and we know rose gardens aren't complete without their thorns. The whole idea that life is supposed to be without pain was just that, an idea, and not based on any more solid reality than other ideas. Without an idea about some other way that life is supposed to be that we are comparing our experience to, all that is left are the facts of the situation. We will always still have a preference for a lack of pain in our lives, for ourselves and for others, but we no longer need life to conform to our preferences. If it conforms, we enjoy that, if it doesn't, we can enjoy that as well and find where it leads us in terms of new directions and new input into our life story.

This kind of acceptance and enjoyment of whatever life gives us does not limit our ability to create the life of our dreams. In fact, it seems to actually open up our creativity to new levels. We are able to see possibilities for ourselves and our world that may never have been visible before when we were limiting our perception so drastically. Now we can see all that is possible without our attachment to whether these possibilities become reality or not and we are freer to take action on them if we are so inclined.

Our actions seem to carry a new effectiveness now, but results are completely outside of our control. For instance, having seen the wonderful array of possibilities that are available to us at any moment, we might then choose one of those possibilities and take an action that moves us in our chosen direction. If mind were to become active in this, it would assume that the action was taken to achieve a particular result and become attached to achieving that result. Without paying attention to mind's noise, what is really happening is that out of the infinite possibilities of one moment, a particular action has occurred, and then the next moment comes and the range of possibilities still stays wide open. That action will change the range of possibilities (not narrow it—change it) and the next moment will offer something else to respond to.

In this way we flow along in the present moment. Mind wants to always narrow the range of possibilities. Having taken one action, it then wants to attach to a particular result happening from that action and to manipulate life into getting that result. This of course is a recipe for unhappiness. As we relax and let results come from a more naturally free-flowing process, the unhappiness has vanished. We no longer need to control life into meeting our specifications. Life becomes much more fun, much lighter. Whatever happens is just what happens, nothing more. We no longer have to work at being a particular kind of person, to conform to an idea of what a good person looks like. We are also always free to revert to our old way of living at any time. There is somehow an inherent perfection even within our human imperfection. This is not something that we need to strive for. This is something that is already here, already done, always available.

This may perhaps sound like license to behave badly, and it would be if it were taken only as an idea being professed by the mind. Mind would take it to mean that it can do anything it pleases. But actually, it is permission to love that part of ourselves which might want to behave badly. It is an invitation to not be afraid of that part of ourselves and try to discipline and manipulate it, but instead to embrace that part within our wholeness. This then naturally alleviates the need for us to keep acting on our worst tendencies. We had only needed to act out these tendencies if we had no other way to bring attention to the parts of ourselves needing inclusion, or to the aspects of our collective human condition that we had not yet embraced.

My personal experience of working with my own tendencies has shown me that there is generally a seeking of comfort at the core of my patterns and I see this as one of the basic urges of the human condition. We have a need to comfort ourselves, to have the comforts of home and a full belly. How can we even relax enough to be able to be a spiritual person if we are not at least comfortable? But can this need for comfort be satisfied by seeking it in this way? Does my own habit of eating comfort foods really make me comfortable? Does having a warm house, hot and cold running water, nice cars and all the conveniences of modern life alleviate this basic human urge towards comfort? It seems obvious that the answers are all no. Although our mentally or emotionally generated comfort-seeking behaviors work for a moment, we are then uncomfortable again, seeking again the next elusive idea of comfort. Actual biological need for warmth or real hunger for food do exist as a reality also, but are so seldom felt in our current lifestyles. The emotional/psychological process of comfort-seeking seems to replace it in our modern day-to-day experience. Interestingly, the long term effect of our modern comfort-seeking lifestyle naturally leads us to the new discomfort of global warming. Similarly, eating for comfort may bring on the discomfort of being overweight or the hardship of feeling unhealthy from improper foods.

So let us use this human urge towards personal comfort as an example of completeness and incompleteness enjoying each other. By accepting the gift of awareness that eating for comfort, for instance, brings us, we can focus our attention on what it is that we really want. We look into what this comfort is that is wanted, but we don't engage our mind's figuring-out process. Instead we just see the comfort seeking for the thought-based process that it is, by looking right into the depths of it and seeing the ideas that it is comprised of and feeling the feelings that the ideas spring from. Sometimes this can be all it takes, although it may over time be felt as a process as we slowly hone in on it. Seeing through the unreality of the ideas behind our conditioned behaviors is sometimes all it takes because we can see that they aren't based on anything true. Sometimes we can also simply and consciously release the ideas that we find to be untrue and the feelings that go with them. Or we can accept the whole pattern fully, let it in, and embrace it.

These two approaches sound opposite but they both are not. They both involve relaxing any desire or aversion that we have regarding the matter. Beyond the parameters of real biological hunger or need, it is our hope that we can get rid of any pattern (and its related issues) that keeps that pattern in place. In one way or another, if we relax those activities of wanting something, or pushing something away, then things can revert to their natural state of equilibrium, and we suddenly can enjoy life again. We enjoy whatever life has given us, whether we got what we wanted or not, whether we ate the "right" foods or not, whether our body is the shape we wanted it to be or not.

What would have previously been seen as a problem, is now seen as life asking for our attention to be given to something, and is no longer evidence of our badness or lack of perfection. It is simply life moving in us, life doing what it does. It is not that difficulties and suffering are no longer present, but that they are received relatively calmly as signposts pointing in directions that we need to look, not as evidence of our lack of awakeness.

The enjoyment of what we are, is then able to relax us again if we are willing, and the process continues, but not within our control. There is no fore-knowledge of where it is all going. We have let go of the effort to control, and our reward is just the joy and lightness of living in this way, rather than some particular end result. We are complete each moment, as well as incomplete and in motion, and we are able to enjoy both fully.

Section 6

Love Beyond Belief

"...The minute I heard my first love story,
I started looking for you, not knowing
how blind that was.

Lovers don't finally meet somewhere,
they're in each other all along..."

Rumi, "The Music Master" [20]

"Love cares not for the me, it cares only for that which
is true, undivided and whole. When the me dissolves,
when it surrenders itself to a unity far greater than
anything the mind can comprehend, that is Love."

Adyashanti [21]

Chapter 21

Love as the One That is Everywhere

I use the word love with some trepidation. It has so many definitions and variations of meaning. We love our sweethearts, our spouses, our children, our friends, and we love God, and it has been up to us to figure out what we mean by love, and what it means to others. "Love Beyond Belief" and "Love Beyond Reason" were some of the working titles of this book along the way. This was changed when I realized that those particular titles were being used by the paperback romance writers! This illustrates the problem with using the word. As a society, we equate the word love with romance and all of the pleasures and difficulties related to our intimate relationships.

Too often what we end up meaning when we say that we love someone is that we have attached ourselves to them in ways that have more to do with emotional security than with awakening. What has so often been called love is something that feeds the endless agendas of the mind-made self, pretending it can make life safe or good. The failure of this mind-made version of love to do that is demonstrated by our divorce rate and our familial abuse statistics. Too often what our society calls love has become a power dynamic between individuals, sometimes subtle (unintentional manipulations of others) and sometimes not so subtle (verbal or physical force).

Let us consider another way of using the word love, so that we can make a distinction between the love that is wielded as a tool of the mind-made self and the Love that exists before and beyond the personal self and its agendas, for which I will henceforth use a capital L. My own experience is that Love is an oceanic field that the separate self seems to fall into when it lets go of itself. I say "seems" because that field is ever-present and there is actually no movement in the falling. But the separate self experiences it that way because when it was busy maintaining its constructed world and identity, the oceanic field of Love was not at first visible. It seems to become visible along the way. As the constructed world of the separate self relaxes, what lies behind and beyond it becomes palpably real. We begin to see the Love that is everywhere, and we begin to move and interact with it and enjoy it.

The Bible makes the statement that God is Love. This clearly points to the experience of seeing everything everywhere appearing as an expression of Love. Though Love is expressed in many different ways, it appears as essentially one thing, coming through many forms. This Love is the same as the oneness that we have discussed earlier. This Love is where we are all connected, whether we like it or not. This Love is the life that feeds us through our food, blooms in the flowers, and crashes in the thunder. It also gives us our bodies when we are conceived and takes them away when they are worn out. It is what brings us our troubles and our calamities, as well as the pleasures and joys of our living.

As the final barriers we have held up against Love fall, we begin to realize that it is not that we are enjoying living in a field of oceanic Love, but that we actually ARE that field. The only things that made it seem otherwise were the mental constructs that we had built up about who we were and what was going on. Without those, we can actually experience in each moment the one life, inside and around us, as one thing, one life, one Love.

The Wedding Feast

When minds rule us
They see a world
Filled with intractable problems
Straining to survive, doubtful of surviving
The onslaught of human life.

But Love would rule the world
And then all of what is seen
ALL of This
Becomes Love's invitation to our hearts.

Love invites us to a wedding feast
In every battleground, in every sickness, in every
famine
We are being beckoned to embrace
Swirling images of death and destruction.
Becoming our completion
As they are embraced in the Heart
Of the world.
In us.

We are both the birthing and the dying at once.
This is a stage, fashioned to discomfort us,
to awaken our hearts
into letting Love take us.

The richness of what we Are
As we include the world
Is only the beginning of what Love would show us.

Without resistance,
We have just gained entrance to the wedding feast
And find with surprise
That we ourselves are the Bride.

Chapter 22

Love Beyond Reason

This Love is not something that we can put in our pocket and keep for ourselves. This Love is larger than the person who would want to keep it. What we started out wanting to acquire for ourselves, has absorbed the small and needy self into its embrace. Instead of having achieved or acquired anything, we are left with both nothing and everything. We have nothing to keep for ourselves or to use to enhance ourselves, but through letting go of that old agenda what has happened is that we have found who we really were all the time, and the feel of it is like the most overwhelming love affair of all time.

We find ourselves in love with life, joined with life and all the nuances and beings that appear in it with no exceptions. All are equal in this Love. It is completely beyond comprehension by the limited mind-made self. It doesn't even make sense in that world. How could I love that speck of dirt on my glasses, and yet, inexplicably, the Love is there. How could I love that imperfect and fallible person, and yet, the Love is there. We find ourselves immersed in this oceanic Love, not requiring anything to be different because of our personal preferences or discomforts. This doesn't have anything to do with personal preferences or individual discomforts. This is the essential nature of everything just simply being what it already is: Love. The difference is just that now we can see it around us and in us, and we feel ourselves to be that Love.

Interacting with our world and all the beings in it, then becomes something completely different than our old agendas where we were looking out for number one in so many ways. One of the little things about this that brought laughter came from driving in the San Francisco Bay Area traffic, which can sometimes be very slow and congested. The world of the personal self dictated that if I got a red light or other traffic blockage, that it then was cause for a subtle movement of disappointment or frustration, whereas if somebody else got a red light so that I could go, then that was cause for ease and good feelings. Now that has been turned on its head. Now there is no visible advantage about which person should be getting the red and green lights, because there is a lack of distinction being made. Somehow, no longer is my getting to my destination sooner more important than the other person getting to their destination. There is nothing magnanimous about it, it just appears as fact. Surprisingly, I still get where I am going on time! Now this may seem a strange illustration in a chapter on Love, but this losing of the assumed importance of the agendas of the personal self, is actually a movement of Love as it meets the everyday world.

In human love, such as may be between marriage partners, there is often also a melding of the edges of self-importance, and our spouse's well-being may feel as important as our own, as may also the well-being of our children. So this experience with traffic is not so foreign, but is an extension of that willingness to let go of our self importance, and extend the circle of our Love to let the whole world in. To take Love to this extent cannot really come from a reasonably made decision to do so, because the rational thought process just can't go there. To extend the circle of Love to this extent can't come from the mind's personal agendas at all, but instead comes from outside of them, coming to, not from, the experience that the individual is having. The role of the individual then is simply to allow space for this Love to penetrate into it, and to express itself through the human being without the mind-made agendas getting in the way.

Once this is experienced, one will naturally tend towards a way of living that is informed by this experience of Love and which expresses that Love in the world. This can take myriad forms, as many as there are people, reflecting our differences as individuals. Our unique personal selves now have the job of acclimatizing themselves to this new role, to serve this Love with their down-to-earth skills and abilities. Each person will express this Love in their own distinct way based on their situations, skills, experiences, gifts, and so forth. This expression may bring to fruition the life work that people have been doing all along, or it may introduce something totally new into people's lives and very much surprise them. Love expressing itself can also sometimes go against the inclinations of the separate self, and bring up any remaining core content which may still constrict the person's life.

Many experiences described in this book are about the patterns of my own unfolding and may or may not describe anything universally applicable or useful to you. Of course each person must work through their own unique versions of these things, but the Love that is now available to lead us through our version of this journey carries us forward. This Love is what we have always wanted and now it is found to have been here all the time. Now, without reason, we are on our way to becoming an expression of Love, living here in the midst of our down-to-earth, perhaps totally mundane lives. We have been united with the essential source that nourishes us, and we thrive through connection and identification with this Love and through the abundantly overflowing resources of a world that now is no longer separate from us.

Whether or not there has been a particular moment where we have consciously dedicated our lives to something beyond ourselves, somehow now that dedication has simply occurred. We can now be fed from this unbelievably generous fountain of life energy that seems to spontaneously meet our needs in a fuller way than if we had known to ask for specific things. Now the outgoing energy of our lives has found a natural flow into expression. This is not to say that difficulties never arise. There is simply an acceptance of those experiences as life's way to guide us through its deeper agenda of awakening. Our task now is to stay, as much as possible, out of the way of Love living in us and through us, as who we are.

This does not mean that our lives will look any particular way or follow any preconceived pattern. We can't know what our lives will look like. We can't even know that they will look spiritual according to any ideas about what spiritual people are like. While some people experience relatively minor outer changes in their lives, others experience the falling away of major aspects of their lives which didn't allow Love to have expression. For some people, there seem to be particular tasks that Love wants done in the world which they are particularly suited to accomplish. This will be felt as life purpose and the resources and connections that are needed will tend to fall into place with amazing synchronicity. For some there will be a continuing lack of clarity about what to do in terms of worldly life. This can be a time of investigating but not being bound by the personality tendencies that constrict the life flow or cause it to look like a problem that the future is unknown, and to open up to one's unique gifts.

The outcome of our letting Love come to life in and through us is that our old mind-made selves now live on the periphery of who we are, not really knowing what is going to happen next. This enlivens our experience of life enormously, but can sometimes feel like having made some ultimate sacrifice. The funny thing is that we didn't really sacrifice anything. Life really was one big mystery all along; we just had blocked that out and tried to make life look safer and more predictable than it really was. Now we realize that we don't and can't know what the future holds, it can open wide the range of possibilities for what can happen in our lives, because we won't be limiting ourselves with our thoughts.

The times of not knowing are so often seen as something to get through and get out of, but to live there permanently is what is being asked of us. It is a place of rich and potent aliveness. The incredible anything-can-happen openness that is so fertile with possibility is not a problem to be solved by the mind. This is exactly where Love flourishes, and where we interfere less with Love's own agenda. This is the place that Love, the universal oneness that we truly are, is most able to express itself in the world. It is where our lives are generated by Love, without our minds having to figure out first what needs to be done. This essential openness where we suspend our personal agendas and ideas is like the infinite wellspring from which spontaneous activity can flow. Our actions then happen in a way where we find ourselves in each moment knowing what to do, and then whatever we do, our doing magically fits with a scenario larger than our personal knowing could ever comprehend.

Love's own agenda in the world is no longer constrained by our personal baggage and we have the opportunity to function in each moment as the hands and feet of this incredible and divine source of life energy. It turns out that our human limitations are not as confining as they once appeared to be. Life opens up as we encounter it, showing us the way forward. The incredible vibrancy of the world around us sustains us generously in its own way and the process appears as a constant miracle. We are free to enjoy life as it is, free to take whatever action flows from us as an expression of Love in the world.

Our actions no longer demand particular results because neither the actions nor any results from them are our own. We may never know which of our actions might have made a difference in the saving of our beloved planet, for example. We don't need to know. We are each moment finished with our work and yet Love still may move us again and again into new activities and new ways of interacting with our world according to its own agenda. We give ourselves over to Love, and trust that it knows better than we do when we are needed to actively get things done, when it is best to remain still, when to pray and when to dance.

We have put ourselves into a dangerous world situation by remaining so long identified with our bundles of mind's ideas, rather than with the Love that is who we truly are. Although practical activities like social service, education, activism for good causes, peace promoting activities, political organizing, etc. have their place in healing the formidable rifts and evident problems in our world, Love's agenda seems to emphasize that we first must penetrate to the core of this question of identity. We each must follow our own unique way to do this. Some of my own experiences as reported in this book may not be directly applicable for people from different backgrounds, but there appears to be a universal process that is hidden behind whatever cultural and personality trappings we are placing on it. It is a process that spans many thousands of years of the human experience, and comes to us today as one way that our lives can truly have something of value to offer our world situation.

Take what is useful and usable from this book, and leave the rest. Extrapolate from all that has been said in this book to find your own way within this dynamic evolutionary process that we have been calling spiritual awakening. Whether you are following a traditional religious path or searching amongst today's alternatives, the way is open for you. Whenever you are ready, you are always welcome into this "life beyond belief". It is being offered to us each moment, right here in the midst of our down-to-earth ordinary lives. As you make room for Love to begin to live and act in you, together we will see where it takes us.

"Therefore, I tell you, don't be anxious for your life: what you will eat, or what you will drink or what you will wear. Which of you, by being anxious, can add anything to the measure of your life?

Consider the lilies of the field, how they grow. They don't toil, neither do they spin, yet I tell you that even Solomon in all his glory was not dressed like one of these. If Love so clothes the grass of the field, which today exists, and tomorrow is thrown into the oven, won't it also clothe you? Therefore don't be anxious, saying, 'What will we eat?', 'What will we drink?' or, 'With what will we be clothed?' But seek first the Kingdom of Heaven; and then all these things will be given to you." 22

Giving and Being Given

Action flowing
from our fingertips,
from our beings,
like our lifeblood
poured out as Love
to the world.

Renewing endlessly also
from the center of the world,
from the center of everything.
The energy flows
constantly back to us
like a perpetual meal
of divine nourishment
provided by Life itself.

Caring for our world,
caring for each other
we endlessly move
in cycles
always carrying
Love's stillness
into Life,
and bearing
Life's vitality
back into Love.

Ending and Beginning Together

Standing still
the way opens naturally,
flows forward.
This moment
carries through all the changes,
unmoving,
like us.

Choices happen and disappear,
Full becomes empty
While empty becomes full,
And we are satisfied
Finding both the same.

This writing...
This fullness soaring as words
that speak
a thousand ways incompletely
that which cannot be spoken,
ends and begins
in the everyday motions
of simple living.

Paying our bills,
weeding our garden,
walking to the store,
We are home again
where we started.
This is it! It was Here all along.

Afterword

As this book is being readied for printing, it is eight months since the original writing was finished and life has not been standing still. The life experiences that have come along are pointing me towards further exploration into the emotional root material from which the mental conditioning arises, and towards new ways of everyday living that are more fully grounded in the physical body and its wisdom.

Exploring deeply in this territory inevitably leads to the necessity of meeting our core emotional foundations and our physical body's symptoms and pains with the same equanimity with which we have come to view our thought processes. In the end nothing can be left out. This means embracing and including *all* of it, even the things we least want to feel, and doing so with compassion for ourselves and for the whole of humanity. A wonderful recent discovery in my own journey has been Michael Brown,[23] who has established *The Presence Process*, a method for allowing core emotional content and physical symptoms to clear through entering into present moment awareness. I recommend his book to those of you who may now also be exploring in this territory with me.

All this is obviously very connected to everything in *Life Beyond Belief* but I felt that this continued exploration may deserve a book of its own. I promise to keep writing, and to share the journey forward from here as it unfolds. The book that you hold in your hands seemed to just happen, pulling me along with its own momentum. I simply made space for it in my life. I will continue to do that, and we will see what will happen next.

It could be that this book happened because I wished that others had left more signposts to follow in bringing spiritual realization down into the very details of everyday life. Or it could be that the book is here to disperse a bit of our culture's fantasies about awakening as an end-point without realizing how much it is also a beginning.

Awakening isn't about getting out of the sometimes mundane and sometimes very painful world of human experience. It is about being willing to go all the way into and through all of the core content of being our human selves and at the same time staying in touch with the purity of our true nature. It is a matter of fully living out our stories, knowing fully what they are, and yet shrinking from nothing. We can then begin to have our down-to-earth humanness be an offering, and to value it as a most precious gift that life has given us, enabling us to become a bridge across the *seeming* expanse between heaven and earth.

Notes

1. Excerpt from the poem *Music Master*, by Jelaladdin Rumi, a prolific Persian poet of the 13th century, *The Essential Rumi* (Edison, New Jersey: Castle Books, 1995), translated by Coleman Barks, p. 106.

2. Adyashanti, *My Secret is Silence*, (Los Gatos, California: Open Gate Publishing, 2003), p. 85.

3. It has become increasingly clear to me that by taking birth we are inherently honoring what the human experience can offer us. Our stories and experiences enhance our awakeness through broadening it and deepening it. Otherwise we wouldn't have bothered to come here in the first place! Taking birth is deciding to learn from the world of story and of experience. It's not that I can personally remember deciding to be born, it's just that the whole human experience, and all the discomforts in it, begins to make sense to me when looked at from this perspective.

4. I first heard the term "mind-made self" used by Eckhart Tolle in *The Power of Now*. I am not

certain if he first coined the term, but I feel it is an excellent way to name the bundle of ideas that we gather up about ourselves in the course of our formative years, and thereafter generally identify with as "me."

5.   The Findhorn Foundation is a spiritual community in northern Scotland founded in 1962 by Eileen Caddy, Peter Caddy and Dorothy MacLean. It is still thriving today, though none of the founders are still living. Its work is based on the values of planetary service, co-creation with nature and attunement to the divinity within all beings. (www.findhorn.org)

6.   *The Power of Now* was the first book written by Eckhart Tolle. It tells a little bit of Eckhart's personal story and develops in depth his basic teaching. I recommend it highly.

7.   A koan is a question in the Zen Buddhist tradition that a master asks a student to ponder as a way of stopping the mind. Questions like "what is the sound of one hand clapping" are not answerable by the mind and lead the student into areas of themselves that are outside the rational mind, in search of an answer to such an illogical question. I notice that life naturally gives us koans all the time in the course of everyday life.

8.   Adyashanti is a spiritual teacher, a native of California and an author of several books. Adyashanti's non-dual teachings have been compared to those of the early Zen masters and Advaita Vedanta sages. Expressing both the infinite possibilities and the ordinary simplicity of a spiritually realized life, Adyashanti's teachings are directed to those who are sincerely called to

awaken to their true nature and to embody this life-changing realization.

9. "Embodiment" is a word that I first heard used by Adyashanti to refer to the process of learning how to actually live the realization of our true nature in the midst of everyday life. Its reference to body is apt because it is about bringing transcendent beingness into the physical world of the body, its activities, and its well-being, as well as the mental and emotional aspects of ourselves.

10. Adyashanti, *My Secret is Silence*, p.1.

11. Eckhart Tolle, *The Power of Now* (Vancouver, Canada: Namaste Publishing, 1997, and Novato, California: New World Library, 1999), p. 68.

12. Written over 2000 years ago, the *Tao Te Ching* is the most widely known ancient Chinese classic in the West and has many translators. The book expounds on many subjects, one of which is "effortless effort," which is also referred to as "non-action." According to the Tao Te Ching, through perfect non-action, nothing is left undone.

13. Eckhart Tolle, *The Power of Now*, p. 158.

14. Adyashanti, *My Secret is Silence*, p.5.

15. Eckhart Tolle, *The Power of Now*, p. 68.

16. Adyashanti, *My Secret is Silence*, p. 36.

17. In 1990, Mihaly Csikszentmihalyi wrote *Flow: The Psychology of Optimal Experience* (New York: Harper Collins, 1990) in which he extensively

discussed the phenomenon of "flow." He has since written many other books related to the subject, and developed his ideas at length. Other writers also develop related ideas in interesting directions. I particularly enjoy the writings of Tim Gallway, whose first book was *The Inner Game of Tennis* (New York: Random House, 1974). He wrote many other wonderful "inner game" books, applying his ideas to many human activities, not only to sports. The central theme of this body of writing is about there being a state of "flow" we can enter that allows us to utilize strengths and abilities that we would not otherwise have.

18. Joseph John Campbell (1904-1987) was an American professor, author and orator best known for his work in the fields of mythology and comparative religion. "Follow your bliss" was a phrase that he distilled from his broad, lifelong study of humanity and used to encapsulate his advice for living. I highly recommend a well-known film that he made at the end of his life, *Joseph Campbell and The Power of Myth, with Bill Moyers*, to anyone who has not already seen it.

19. Jelaluddin Rumi, translated by Coleman Barks, *The Essential Rumi*, p. 109.

20. Jelaluddin Rumi, translated by Coleman Barks, *The Essential Rumi*, p. 106.

21. Adyashanti, *The Impact of Awakening: Excerpts from the Teachings of Adyashanti*, p. 81-82.

22. Paraphrased and excerpted from Matthew 6:25-31 and Luke 12:22-31, *American Standard Bible*.

23. Michael Brown, *The Presence Process, A Healing Journey into Present Moment Awareness*, (Vancouver, Canada: Namaste Publishing, and New York: Beaufort Books, 2005).

Selected Bibliography

I list here only the writings produced by those people who have most closely affected my spiritual journey, and even then I have not tried to list their complete works. This is by no means an all-inclusive record of all the works and sources that have influenced me over the years. For a longer list of interesting reading along the lines of this book, please visit my Web site www.wideawakeliving.com. You will find there a "recommended reading list" and a "links" page for connecting to the Web sites of the respective authors.

Adyashanti. *The Impact of Awakening: Excerpts from the Teachings of Adyashanti.* Los Gatos, California: Open Gate Publishing, 2000.

_____. *My Secret is Silence: Poetry and Sayings of Adyashanti.* Los Gatos, California: Open Gate Publishing, 2003.

_____. *Emptiness Dancing.* Los Gatos, California: Open Gate Publishing, 2004.

Brown, Michael. *The Presence Process, A Healing Journey Into Present Moment Awareness.* Vancouver,

Canada: Namaste Publishing, and New York: Beaufort Books, 2005.

Caddy, Eileen. *God Spoke to Me*. 3d ed., Scotland: Findhorn Press, 1992.

MacLean, Dorothy. *To Hear the Angels Sing: An Odyssey of Co-Creation with the Devic Kingdom*. Herndon, Virginia: Lindisfarne Books, 1994.

MacLean, Dorothy and Kathy Thormod. *To Honor the Earth: Reflections on Living in Harmony with Nature*. New York: HarperCollins, 1991.

Moss, Richard, MD. *The I That is We, Awakening to Higher Energies Through Unconditional Love*. Berkeley, California: Celestial Arts, 1981.

_____. *Mandala of Being, Discovering the Power of Awareness*. Novato, California: New World Library, 2007.

Rumi, Jelaluddin. Translated by Coleman Barks. *The Essential Rumi*. Edison, New Jersey: Castle Books, 1995.

Tolle, Eckhart. *The Power of Now*. Vancouver, Canada: Namaste Publishing, 1997, and Novato, California: New World Library, 1999.

_____. *Practicing the Power of Now*. Vancouver, Canada: Namaste Publishing, and Novato, California: New World Library, 2001.

_____. *Stillness Speaks*. Vancouver, Canada: Namaste Publishing, and Novato, California: New World Library, 2003.

_____. *A New Earth: Awakening to Your Life's Purpose.* Vancouver, Canada: Namaste Publishing, and New York: The Penguin Group, 2005.

About the Author

ALICE GARDNER lives very much in the mainstream of modern life. She holds a Master of Management degree from Cambridge College, Massachusetts, and has worked as an academic administrator at educational institutions in Brattleboro, Vermont and Palo Alto, California. She volunteers with Open Gate Sangha and mentors an international group of people online and by telephone.

Alice's journey began early in her adult life when she lived seven years at the Findhorn Foundation in Scotland. In the late 80s, she was particularly influenced by the teachings of Richard Moss, and more recently by both Eckhart Tolle and Adyashanti.

After growing up in Connecticut, Alice raised a family in rural Vermont and is now the proud mother of grown children. She especially enjoys country living, nature photography, reading, writing and the great outdoors. She now lives and works in the San Francisco Bay Area of California.

You are invited to visit Alice's Web site,
www.wideawakeliving.com
and subscribe to her monthly
Wide Awake Living Newsletter.

CPSIA information can be obtained at www.ICGtesting.com
Printed in the USA
LVOW072143051011

249324LV00006B/32/A